BLACK MUSIC

Cecil Taylor

Ornette Coleman

Herbie Nichols

Jackie McLean

by **A. B. SPELLMAN**

BLACK

MUSIC

FOUR

LIVES

SCHOCKEN BOOKS · NEW YORK

THIRD PRINTING, 1973

First SCHOCKEN PAPERBACK edition 1970

Originally published under the title
Four Lives in the Bebop Business by Pantheon Books

Copyright © 1966 by A. B. Spellman
Library of Congress Catalog Card No. 76–123365
Published by arrangement with Pantheon Books
Manufactured in the United States of America

CONTENTS

INTRODUCTION

O RNETTE COLEMAN, Cecil Taylor, Herbie Nichols, and Jackie McLean—four profoundly different but closely related lives in the bebop business, that peculiar cross-pollination of show business and serious modern jazz that has developed since the bebop revolution of the Forties. In their collective biographies is a microcosm of the contemporary scene for the black American jazz musician.

Ornette Coleman, the self-taught poor boy from Texas, struggling to find a means of self-expression in the deep South, in California, in New York and in Europe, fired from a carnival band in Natchez, Mississippi, for trying to teach bebop licks to a fellow band member, whipped for a tenor saxophone solo in Baton Rouge, Louisiana, scornfully rejected for his music and manner in Los Angeles, became one of America's most talked-about serious musicians in the 1960's.

Cecil Taylor's route to controversy was entirely different. He was born in the black bourgeoisie (note in his story that even a black servant can be a member of the black bourgeoisie if he can get up the trimmings) in a comfortable Long Island suburb and trained in one of the best musical conservatories on the East Coast; his main musical struggle was to find a method of improvisation that would achieve the proper balance between his training and his roots.

Herbie Nichols and Jackie McLean, on the other hand, began their careers at the opposite ends of the bebop revolution, one discouraged from participating in that revolution, because he refused to become a hipster in the age of hip, the other a teen-age prodigy who became too hip for his own good.

Many currents cross in these pages, the most sinister of which is the gross indifference with which America receives those aspects of Afro-American culture that are not "entertaining." Jazz's entertainment value has decreased as black artists have conscientiously moved out of the realm of folk art and into the realm of high art; and I maintain that much of the jazz music of the last twenty years and some of the jazz of the previous thirty years *is* high art and should be treated with all the dignity that high art deserves. I am not suggesting that alienation, frustration, humiliation, and deprivation are the exclusive property of the jazz musician; certainly the great majority of artists in America are poor and outcast people. But literature, classical music, and the plastic arts are taught from both the appreciative and creative viewpoints in all colleges and many of the high schools of the United States in a blind adulation of European culture, while there is little academic effort at fostering the one art form unique and indigenous to the United States. Furthermore, fortunes can be raised to sponsor prestigious symphonic and operatic societies in any sizable American city: it is of utmost importance that the rich convince themselves that they are "cultured." But serious jazz is left almost exclusively to a few out-of-the-way bars, and is given very little time on the radio and a negligible amount of time on television, so that there is nothing in the average American's life to reorient him toward this most highly developed aspect of Afro-American culture.

Reviewing the experiences of the people this book deals with, it is difficult to understand how they survived at all as artists. How *does* Cecil Taylor face those half-upright pianos to which he is forced to accommodate his difficult and complex music? How *did* Jackie McLean keep his mind open to growth in those years when he used heroin to blot out the demons who inhabit those days and nights of the black jazz artist? Why *didn't* Ornette Coleman go back to Texas and become a rhythm-and-blues tenor saxophonist after receiving only scorn and hatred from a community of modern musicians, to become a part of which he had struggled through the length and breadth of the deep South? And poor, disillusioned Herbie Nichols, a great pianist and composer of whom very few of even the most ardent jazz enthusiasts have heard, died without recognition despite years of trying to achieve a breakthrough.

Here, in Herbie Nichols' life, is exemplified another theme of this book: the capriciousness of the jazz industry. No pianist as obviously beautiful and original as Herbie Nichols could be as absolutely unsalable as the record companies and nightclub owners thought that Herbie was; yet there he was, hidden away in the Bronx without a dime, dying of old age at forty-four, having been forced for years to waste his considerable talent playing dated music.

With Jackie McLean this capriciousness takes on a different form. For example, McLean has, at times, been over-recorded because his situation forced him to take any record date offered to him just to make a payday. He made many such "pickup" records (he calls them "stews"), which had some value when they were made but are relatively un-interesting to listen to now. This is not an uncommon practice among companies specializing in recording jazz: many of them keep a stable of musicians, who they know have diffi-cult personal problems, to assure them of a stream of com-petently made but cheaply produced records.

If managers of record companies and club owners ap-pear as villains in these pages, it is because they are; blame-less villains, perhaps, but villains nonetheless. They are, of course, businessmen, and the commercial value of a group or musician is their foremost consideration. That a Dave Bru-beck can be approaching millionaire status while Cecil Tay-lor, Jackie McLean, and Ornette Coleman are relative pau-pers is, from my perspective, outrageous; but why be naive? Has it ever been different? Did not the Original Dixie-land Jazz Band make many times the money of Jelly Roll Morton's Red Hot Peppers? It is a critical assumption these days that Benny Goodman took much of his group approach from Fletcher Henderson's innovations, and Goodman is now one of America's wealthiest musicians; Henderson died as broken and frustrated as Herbie Nichols. Black musicians such as Louis Armstrong who made fortunes playing jazz are rare; but even Louis Armstrong, giant that he is, could never have made it so far without including blatant Uncle Tomism in his act (viz.: Armstrong's role in the old "all colored cast" movie *Cabin in the Sky*). The dollar is king in the bebop business, as it is in any business, and there is no precedent for expecting club owners to feel responsible for fostering cul-ture by hiring the most important groups if they are not convinced that those groups will make money for them. Certainly, some of the new music can make (and has made) money for the nightclubs, but there is little doubt in my mind that the new music has outgrown the old scene.

Some readers may wonder why I have chosen these four lives to telescope the bebop business. Couldn't the same point be made with four other lives? Well, yes and no. Many of the experiences related in this book are common to most black modern jazz musicians, and quite a few of these situations befall some white jazz musicians as well. But important people should be talked about first, and all these men are that.

Ornette Coleman and Cecil Taylor are two of the three most important new jazz musicians of the decade (John Coltrane, the third, is not included because he did not want to be), and the full scope of their influence still has not been fully realized. (This is particularly true of Cecil Taylor.) There were indeed some musicians—Charlie Mingus, for example—who were trying to broaden the mainstream of the Fifties before the advent of Taylor and Coleman; but they were the first two musicians to appear on the scene who placed themselves totally outside the mainstream and had the temerity to suggest that all the assumptions of hard and cool bop would have to be overhauled before the individual voice could once again replace the cliché in jazz.

Since the Coleman-Coltrane-Taylor assault, the number of musicians committed to the new music has grown to well over a hundred, and I hear new names weekly. The best of the old-guard leaders, men such as Max Roach, Miles Davis, and, of course, Jackie McLean, hire these young revolutionists, with the result that their own music has taken on new dimensions. Cecil's and Ornette's experiences in the bebop business have been different from the experiences of those who have conformed to the patterns of an essentially nonconformist scene.

Jackie McLean is important because he has been among the very top men on the alto saxophone for more than ten years. He has been active in jazz for more than fifteen, and he has been growing all this time, so that his playing includes much of what has happened in jazz in these fifteen years. Jackie also knows better than anyone else I can think of what life in the bebop business is like. He has lived it all, and he has seen it lived. He has known geniuses who never got out of Harlem, and he has known mediocre musicians who have made it big.

Herbie Nichols is important not only because of the music he made but also because of the music he did not make. Let me suggest that any reader interested enough to read Herbie's story petition Blue Note records for a copy of the LP *The Herbie Nichols Trio* and discover for himself the tremendous unrealized potential of this unhappy musician.

I met Herbie Nichols only four times. The first time was at a loft party in New York City where he was playing a benefit with saxophonist Archie Shepp. The second time was during a day of live broadcasting at WBAI-FM, where Herbie was my guest for a half-hour program of his music. He was uncomfortable on that occasion, and I had not been able to find a drummer and bassist to accompany him. I kept trying to get him to open up—to play faster tunes longer, and to talk about himself—but he was too tight, and did not make a good impression on the listeners. When I played Herbie's records the next day, many of them could not believe that it was the same man. Our last two meetings were at his sister's apartment in the Bronx, where I conducted the interviews that went into this book. Obviously, I cannot say that I knew him intimately; but the disillusionment in Herbie's face, voice, and demeanor could not have been clearer to me if I had known him for twenty years.

I have known Cecil Taylor since I started hitchhiking from Washington, D.C., where I was a student at Howard University, to New York in the late Fifties to catch his concerts. He is an erudite and articulate man whose interests range far beyond music.

I have known Ornette Coleman and many of the musicians who have played with him since his arrival in New York in 1959. Ornette, perhaps more than any other modern jazz musician, is firmly rooted in the tradition of his people. Once past his radical innovations in tone and tonality, one can hear shuffles, stomps, hollers, and certainly blues in his music. To put it another way, once you get past the complexity of it, this is relatively simple music; and the same can be said of Ornette's personality. He moves from point to point in a straight line, but these lines, put together, form a zigzag course. Ornette is a superior craftsman in the same sense that blues singer Lightnin' Hopkins is; and he does not value music for the sake of artifice but for what it can get off his chest.

Jackie McLean is a more pragmatic and worldly man. His experience has been largely in the streets, and his curiosity is directed toward trying to understand how the social world is put together and how it may be improved. He reads constantly, but he is more likely to read a book on the success and failure of Toussaint L'Ouverture's Haitian revolution than one on esthetics.

During the brief period when he worked there, Jackie's efforts at HARYOU-ACT in Harlem proved highly effective. He has been so much "in the life" that the youngsters respected him as they never respect professional social workers. Any Harlem teen-ager who has an interest in playing music would be proud to have Jackie McLean for a teacher, and some of the agency's most antisocial charges have accepted Jackie's advice to avoid making the same mistakes that he made in his youth.

These, then, are the four lives treated in this book. I *could* have chosen four others, but frankly these are four of my favorite musicians and men; and, like most people, I tend to satisfy my subjective instincts first.

Most of the material included in these pages is taken from interviews that I recorded, either in my home or in the homes of the men who contributed to this work. The tapes were then transcribed, and altogether came to nearly five hundred pages of firsthand information; the essence of that material forms the body of this book.

I have tried to let the musicians speak for themselves as much as possible. It would have been my preference to see published four autobiographies to give as clear a picture as possible of what these musicians think of their own lives. I have shifted and spliced, and moved their ideas around to put them in their most advantageous places, but I have not put words in their mouths. They have enough of their own.

July 1966
New York

I. CECIL TAYLOR

J EANNE PHILLIPS is a black woman who has devoted much of her adult life to modern jazz. She is
particular and serious, and is frequently seen in her large,
outlandishly tasteful hats at those coffee shops and concert
halls, bars, basements, and lofts where that long, loud, dis-
cordant, often unmeasured but usually powerful jazz that the
critics have named, in dismay, the "New Thing," is played.
Jeanne is not one of those female camp followers who try to
out-sit each other in the jazz clubs in the early hours of the
morning for the honor of going home with the trumpet
player but, rather, a committed woman whose opinions are
valued and whose barbs are feared by those musicians and
critics who know her. Miss Phillips is one of a relatively
small number of people who have entry into the musicians'
gallery at the jazz clubs. She exemplifies perfectly that
growing group of new jazz loyalists who feel, with reason,
that history has deposited the vital culture of these times in
their corner.

Miss Phillips was talking about the great interest that some of the more notable contemporary composers have shown in modern jazz, specifically in pianist Cecil Taylor.

"It's sad—the only true history of America is recorded in its music. The music says what's really happening here. And now that the Negro has become more educated and the Negro musician has learned all the techniques of European classical music, then it's the Negro musician who keeps the culture of America alive. Because America doesn't have any other culture of its own, except what the Negro gave it and what it borrowed from Europe, and I think Europe is dead. All these cats with their electronic stuff—how the hell is a machine going to make music? No more than a washing machine does when it's operating. You hear sounds all day long, and unless they're incorporated correctly by men, there ain't no music.

"As far as music per se is concerned, Cecil is one of the most prominent musicians that Western civilization has, and they know it. I go a lot of places, I always arrange to be around, and I listen. For musical stimulation and creativity, Cecil is where it is, and they're trying to find out about the music, how it's constructed. They want the key. Cecil has the key, that's who has the key. And it's the same word they use to describe music made by Muddy Waters. It's all blues, all of it. The classical music of our times is jazz."

For "classical," read "serious," and we are into the growing polarization of interests that characterizes this era of overcommunication. Since the bebop revolution of the Forties, jazz musicians have been regarding themselves as something other than entertainers, which, apart from a displacement of the great body of jazz in the entertainment industry, has resulted in a forwarding by jazz musicians and the exponents of modern jazz of the principles and roots of jazz improvisation vis-à-vis the contemporary European techniques of composed improvisation by means of chance, graphs, electronic determination, etc.

The incorporation of twentieth-century European techniques with jazz has been pursued chiefly by white musicians, such as Jimmy Giuffre, Paul and Carla Bley, Mike Mantler, and Gunther Schuller, with the result that the formal and technical problems of how to include improvised sections in a dialogue between jazz quartet and string quartet, or how to incorporate a blues line into an improvised tone row, could not be resolved within the old forms, and new forms, neither jazz nor Western, were not created.

The black musicians, such as John Lewis and J. J. Johnson, who were involved in what has been called Third Stream music have been decidedly nineteenth century in their European derivations. They belong to a tradition in jazz in which one first proves oneself capable of playing classical music to show that playing the blues was a matter of choice. This tradition goes back to Jelly Roll Morton, James P. Johnson, and Willie "The Lion" Smith, who once boasted that he could "play Chopin faster than any man alive."

There is only one musician who has, by general agreement even among those who have disliked his music, been able to incorporate all that he wants to take from classical and modern Western composition into his own distinctly individual kind of blues without in the least compromising those blues, and that is Cecil Taylor, a kind of Bartók in reverse.

Taylor is so outstanding in the contemporary musical scene that there is no one to compare him to. Whether he is attacking the keyboard in one of his overwhelming flights of power or coaxing the tenderest blues and ballad lines from it, there is no confusing his playing with any other music. The materials, methods, and traditions that he incorporates into his music are so broadly conceived that he stands squarely astride the musical development of this period. His name may someday be a household word, but he is important enough now to have achieved that status already. Yet Cecil Taylor has so far found the world a hostile place indeed.

CECIL TAYLOR AND ADVERSITY

"Miles Davis plays pretty well for a millionaire."

"Ellington's sixty-five years old. Somebody said, 'Well he sure looks good.' I said, 'Well that's adversity, man.'"

"That piano has developed from my poverty, not having the money to tune it. Certain things have happened to that piano just because I played it."

These statements provide a valuable insight into Cecil Taylor's life and approach to the world. Apart from the kind of adversity that is a daily staple of every black American's life, Taylor sees adversity as being concomitant with artistic integrity, and a fructifying element in his life. America being what it is, adversity is the natural lot of both the artist and the Negro. Cecil can do nothing about his color, but he did not have to choose a career that, by its nature, conflicts directly with commercial success. Modern jazz has developed gradually from social music, and it still has a large popular wing that does not consider its music too serious to compromise. Jazz has a limited-enough popular audience, and the jazz entrepreneurs are extremely careful to be as inoffensive as possible in what they bring to that audience.

That Cecil Taylor has drawn well almost every time he has played in New York does not endear him to nightclub owners. The Five Spot's Joe Termini will not have Cecil for an extended stay, even though it was Cecil who originally established the Five Spot as a home of serious jazz, and even though in his last (at this writing) appearance there, a Monday night, he drew an overflow audience. Sonny Murray, Cecil's drummer for several years, doubts that Cecil has made $50,000 for himself and his group in ten years in the jazz business. Murray says: "I've seen Cecil go to the agents with his project all outlined, and the agents say, 'Oh, you're Cecil Taylor, I've heard of you. Just wait outside a few minutes.' And Cecil sits outside and listens to some cat in the agent's office imitating him, but watering it down, you dig. And I've seen these agents come out and tell Cecil, 'Oh man, I'm sorry, look, come back sometime when I've got more time.' And the other chump, the cat who stole Cecil's shit, gets the contract. Now these are the big-time agents, the agents who book Coltrane and Rollins in ten clubs in the United States every six months.

"Like Termini. He gave Cecil six weeks at the old Five Spot and Cecil drew enormously. He has a beautiful following. So then Termini gives him a Monday night two years later and he draws enormously again. But what Termini doesn't realize, or maybe he doesn't care about, is that Cecil doesn't need the Monday night. He needs the six weeks again. All this frustrates him, all the tricks the agents and the owners play on him. I've seen this."

It is not, then, merely a question of the size of the following. Termini says, "Cecil has always drawn well. There's a group that shows up every time he plays." It's a matter of the nature of the music, and Cecil Taylor simply does not play barroom music.

Termini complains about the length of the sets: "The length of Cecil's tunes has always been a minor hassle between us. When Archie Shepp was playing tenor with Cecil, it was a hassle because the sets were running almost two hours. I tried to get them to let up, to cut the sets short, but Cecil said he couldn't."

Buell Neidlinger, Cecil's bassist for many years, finds the music inherently unsuited to the nightclub owner's uses: "Trying to make a living playing with Cecil is absolutely unbelievable, because there is no economic advantage to playing music like that. It's completely unsalable in the nightclubs because of the fact that each composition lasts, or could last, an hour and a half. Bar owners aren't interested in this, because if there's one thing they hate to see it's a bunch of people sitting around openmouthed with their brains absolutely paralyzed by the music, unable to call for the waiter. They want to sell drinks. But when Cecil's playing, people are likely to tell the waiter to shut up and be still.

"We used to run into this all the time at the Five Spot. For some reason, I guess because I'm white, the owners considered me, like, the one to talk to whenever there was trouble. We'd be playing along for an hour or so and I'd get the old radio signal—the hand across the throat. Cut 'em off! Cut 'em off!

"But you can't. If Igor Stravinsky was sitting down writing, you wouldn't all of a sudden run in and say, 'Stop it, Igor! Like, we want to sell a few drinks!' It's about the same thing. You can't tell Cecil to stop."

Yet, as the owners of New York's Village Vanguard recently learned, Cecil is a moneymaker. Termini says that Cecil "always drew well. He fills the place a whole lot better than a lot of the people who have the reputation of being top drawers do." And Neidlinger estimates Cecil's New York audience—that is, those who will come out regularly to hear him whenever he plays, at two thousand; and "it is growing, and it is almost fanatical."

Termini could give no reason for not hiring Taylor more often. His general attitude was that there is no money in any jazz, because its audience is young and fickle: "I might not have jazz in the future. People seem to like dancing, and I might go into that. The jazz following is just not a commercial popular following. There are well over five hundred jazz musicians in New York, and maybe five clubs that hire jazz musicians.

"Birdland has closed, but that business hasn't spread around like you'd think it would. The jazz audience is made up of young people. The majority of them go through a phase when they're listening to jazz, but then they go on to something else. And after they get married, get jobs, you never see them again. So new ones have to come along to replace the ones who stop coming.

"I don't know. If I lose money, I won't have jazz anymore. Giving up the jazz policy would be throwing away the last ten years."

Termini does not know where the fault is. He agrees with most jazz people that agents do more harm than good, and with most owners that some musicians ask more than the owners can pay. He agrees with most of the younger musicians that the new jazz hasn't had enough exposure to kill the audience.

But Termini's experience is the same as that of the owners of many of the New York clubs that did well with jazz over the years: they all started with nothing, and made their names and fortunes from jazz. Termini's original Five Spot was an ordinary Bowery bar, with a broken-down piano in the corner, before Cecil Taylor was hired in 1956, when it immediately attracted a new crowd of artists, writers, and members of what at that time was commonly referred to as the Uptown Bohemia. The skids went out, the sawdust came off the floor, the prices went up, and the Terminis were soon operating two nightclubs, the Five Spot and the Jazz Gallery. Before Cecil, Termini could not have thought of opening a discothèque. He now has a shiny new room at a better location which is suitable for live or recorded popular music. It is typical of the jazz experience that modern jazz has brought him to this.

Cecil himself sees the financial problems of the new musicians as the result of often willful mismanagement of the new music by the people who command the mechanics of the industry: "Yes, there's a commercial market. I talk to cats like [pianist] Andrew Hill, who goes around, who works around. The people are out there. The people are really and truly out there and they're buying the records, but record companies lie about what's being sold. I get letters every day of the week from people in Detroit. I hear from people in metropolitan areas out in California and other places in the West and Midwest. If I were to go there, it would be just like working for the first time. I met one guy who runs a nightclub outside New York who told me he's been trying to get me for two years, but every time he calls the agency, the agency says I'm not available."

Cecil has worked variously as a delivery man for a Madison Avenue coffee shop, record salesman, cook and dishwasher. He used to work at Macy's at Christmas, putting in all the overtime he could, and live for months on what he'd made. His jazz engagements have averaged about two a year—many in rarely frequented coffee shops for a percentage of the admission receipts—with an occasional festival appearance or concert.

According to Buell Neidlinger, he was once fired from

the Five Spot because a powerful friend of Thelonious
Monk's overheard Norman Mailer praising Cecil's music.
Buell says: "Norman Mailer came in one night while we were
playing and he'd had a lot of drinks. That was while Monk
was working at the Jazz Gallery. So Norman Mailer sat down
for a while and all of a sudden jumped up and said, 'I've just
come from the Jazz Gallery and listening to Monk, and this
guy Cecil Taylor is much better than Monk and all the people
at the Gallery ought to be over here listening to him.'

"That was the end of that gig at the Five Spot, because
they had us out of there without even a week's notice. Joe's
brother came over and said, 'You guys are through Sunday.'
That was on a Thursday."

The problem with not working on a regular basis is not
merely financial; it seriously inhibits the musical development of a band. Buell goes on: "That was too bad because
Dennis [Dennis Charles, a drummer] and I had been with
Cecil on and off for a number of years and we had never
figured out until that period what he was up to. We were just
getting to the point where we could relax on the bandstand to
really make music with Cecil instead of just following along.
We were just getting to the point where we could make a real
contribution. If we'd been together for the whole summer,
the results would have been fantastic.

"But that was the end of that. I had some trouble soon
after and lost my cabaret card, so I couldn't work in nightclubs anymore and Dennis soon went his own way."

For Cecil, the breakup of a band is a far more serious
matter than it is for any other leader, with the exception of
such similarly individualistic composers as Thelonious Monk
and Ornette Coleman. Most of his sidemen admit that it
takes a minimum of three years of steady rehearsal to fully
assimilate his music. Cecil's approach to group improvisation

is so demanding that it usually requires a thorough re-evaluation for the musician. One like Buell Neidlinger, who had no appreciation for any kind of modern music when he started with Cecil, may be said to have been trained from scratch.

It is also true that, until the last two years, Cecil has had trouble getting musicians to play with him. Jimmy Lyons, who plays alto saxophone with him, says that he "has trouble finding drummers who will listen for something else besides that 1–2–3–4," and only three drummers, Dennis Charles, Sonny Murray, and Andrew Cyrille, have ever worked with him for any extended period of time. One of these, Murray, undeveloped when he started rehearsing with Cecil, was even more of an outcast than Taylor was, but he is now considered a major innovator by his contemporaries. It is to Cecil's credit that he heard Sonny's latent talent and had the patience to develop it when nobody else could figure out why Murray was being used. Sonny remembers first meeting Cecil: ". . . at the Cafe Roué, which was one of the first jazz coffee shops in the West Village. The drummers in the business were a little leery of me because my sense of time and rhythm was a little too advanced for them, even though I didn't have it all together. In '56 I was playing one and three on my sock [cymbal], and they used to complain that I wasn't playing on the beat, I mean not a flam-one and flam-two. If I heard myself about to play a cliché, I just wouldn't play it. So one night I was in the Roué and I got up to sit in. The cats never were too happy to play with me, the bass players especially, and the drummers would stand around and put me down. So just as I got up to play, Cecil came in. I saw the musicians packing up their instruments, so I said, 'What are you packing up your instruments for? You really don't dig playing with me that much?' And they said, 'No Sonny, it's not you tonight, it's really not you!' And I said,

'Well who is it then?' And they said, 'It's that cat sitting over there in the corner. We're not going to play with *him*.'

"About this time, another cat came up. He is now just a minor person of the streets, you know. He's nutted out, been in Bellevue. By now, I guess he's lost all interest in music. But at this time he wanted to be a bass player, and he used to follow Cecil around. He was talented. He could have been credited with being one of the first free bass players. He played for only four months, but he played those four months on people's jobs, by walking up and picking up the bass. Cats used to say, 'But you don't know this, and you don't know that.' And he would say, 'I know, but I want to play this bass!' And he would play it.

"So he was in the place and he said to me, 'Don't get up man, like that's my man. That's Cecil Taylor. He's my man and I'm going to tell him to play something.' So I said, 'Does he know that you don't know anything about the bass?' He said, 'He's *glad* I don't know anything about the bass.'

"So when Cecil went to the piano, there I was, prepared to play. I thought, 'Well, the man's probably something like Monk.' So the cat started playing, and I did something, I don't know what I did, but he looked over his shoulder and said, 'Do that again. You've got the will, so the spirits will do it.' I'll never forget that. So I kept going and the other cat was doing hmm–hmm things on the bass and the next thing you know like we had played a whole tune.

"Then Cecil said, 'Thank you' and split. I still don't know what happened."

Such reaction from his contemporaries was typical of Cecil's experience those first years on the New York scene. It was not the same reaction that Ornette Coleman received from musicians and critics, who said that he did not know how to play his instrument. Cecil obviously knew how to do that. It was that Cecil's music was an abrupt challenge to the hard bop music with its ready availability to both performer and listener. Unless Cecil would just go away, music would never be the same, and the musical scene would never be the same.

Murray considers the musicians cowards for refusing to play with Taylor: "He's had a hard time, because the cats are, like, 'runners away.' They didn't have enough faith in themselves to believe they could handle as much music as Cecil plays, which some of them can. Cats like [tenor saxophonist] Archie Shepp, [bassist] Henry Grimes, and Jimmy Lyons have proved that."

But this is one problem that Cecil has solved, or which the generation of musicians that grew up on Cecil Taylor, Ornette Coleman, and John Coltrane has solved for him. Jeanne Phillips remembers seeing some musicians hanging around the bandstand while Cecil was playing a few years ago who seemed at the time too young to be in the nightclub, but who now have gone as musically far out as Taylor.

There was also hostility from more established musicians. Cecil recalls a one-Monday-night stand at Birdland that was attended by Miles Davis, Dizzy Gillespie, Sarah Vaughan, and Erroll Garner: "Miles just cursed and walked out. Dizzy wandered in and out and kept making all kinds of remarks to Sarah, who was in a pretty vicious mood. Miles later put me down in print. The only one who dug the proceedings was Erroll Garner, and that, in a way, was more important to me than what the others said, because Erroll is a pianist, and a great one, and has a great appreciation for keyboard sound."

Jeanne Phillips feels that Cecil is already a major influence: "You look at the situation. Certain musicians were hostile to Cecil, but certain others dug him. An interesting thing is that someone like Monk has Cecil's records. Who knows whether Miles does or not? When Miles first heard Cecil, back in the Fifties, he put him down, right? Well, it's an interesting thing that Miles's present piano player, Herbie Hancock, is trying to go in Cecil's direction, because he thinks that's where the music has to go. And these musicians dig Cecil. Miles's drummer, Tony Williams, does. Tony would rather play with Cecil than with Miles. That would sound strange wouldn't it? But it's a fact.

"Even a musician as great as Eric Dolphy looked forward to the time he could play with Cecil. Eric had all Cecil's records, and his whole thing is that he wanted to play with Cecil. Eric was very tight with me, and he used to say, 'I think I'm learning how to play with Cecil.' He kept on saying this to me because he didn't feel like he could say it to Cecil.

"It was the weirdest thing. Before Eric went to Europe, he told me about a dream he had had. He dreamt he was on the bandstand with Cecil and another clarinet player. I asked him who that was and he said he didn't know. Anyway, he was on the stand with Cecil and he was waiting for his turn to play. He said he kept saying to himself, 'At last, I'm going to play with Cecil.' And before he could play, he fell down dead on the bandstand. This was the last time I talked to him before he went to Europe, and the next thing I heard, Eric had died of a heart attack on the stage in Berlin. It was the weirdest thing."

Perhaps the worst form of adversity that Cecil has experienced in the double alienation of the black artist in America is the alienation from his own, perhaps *former* should be the word, community. This is the result of several factors, including the new serious approach to music that jazzmen took in the Forties. LeRoi Jones wrote of that music: "If only by implication, bebop led jazz into the arena of *art*, one of the most despised terms in the American language. But, as art, or at least as separated from the vertiginous patronization of the parochial term *folk art*, . . . the Negro music of the Forties had pushed its way into a position of serious (if controversial) regard."

The social usage of art implied a certain status that is anything but communal. Though Afro-Americans have arrived at a "serious" music whose principles and features are essentially different from those of Western "serious" music, that it should be "serious" at all negates what Jones calls the functionality of Negro music. All those stereotypical aspects of black American culture for which Negroes are always being criticized and to which music is attached—the penchant for social dancing, the frenetic religiosity—have been, through the release that they offer, mediums of survival, and music has been the medium's medium.

But release is no longer enough. The comforting social groupings created by the church are no longer enough. The jazz musicians who produced bebop in the Forties may be said to have been the artistic vanguard of the dynamic social action that the later decades were to experience, ranging from the court actions of the NAACP all the way to the Watts riots. If the Afro-American had been allowed a similar outlet for the African tradition of, say, sculpture as he was for music, then a Charlie Parker would have created visual images as portentously unbearable to America as Grosz's or Beckmann's or Ensor's were to Germans.

Jazz is a great American art, yet it is treated as a cultural stepchild. It is bad enough that it is performed almost exclusively in bars, yet even this outlet is shrinking to the point of invisibility. There are several reasons for this state of affairs, not the least of which is the set of New York City's cabaret laws, passed under Mayor Fiorello LaGuardia, which taxed and harassed cabarets nearly out of existence in the communications center of the world. These laws are imitated in many of the major urban centers in the country. This factor, combined with the just union wage demands and the emergence of the agent as a middleman, completely killed the possibilities of music and dance in the fifteen-cent-beer bars, with the result that live music was completely out of the reach of even the average *white* Harlem bar owner. And those who could afford it most were the least interested in any new music.

By the arbitrary determination of the jazz industry, the music has been available only to serious students (many of them white) in neutral zones, never played on the radios, especially in black neighborhoods, and never produced in black nightclubs or concert halls unless the names were very big. What jazz jobs there are in the Harlems of America go invariably to the safest performers. And the young musicians who are interested in the new music almost always have to take their music "downtown," in order to find a receptive atmosphere.

In this way, the black jazz musician has had to take his alienation alongside the black poet and painter, and on the occasions when this prodigal music has returned home, the reception has been anything but predictable. The mobile avant-garde jazz performances that LeRoi Jones's Black Arts group put on in the streets of Harlem during the summer of 1965 received a generally favorable audience response, but eggs were thrown at one group. And Archie Shepp, who plays a more gutbucket style of tenor saxophone than most of the new modern tenor saxophone players, received a better welcome at a down-home type bar in Baltimore than he had on most occasions in New York.

The problem is essentially that the young musicians who were interested in playing the new jazz have had to leave their own communities and go to so-called bohemian quarters, where a similar alienation had produced something resembling a consistently sympathetic, if small, audience. Cecil Taylor says, "The alienation happened because of the insurgence of the middlemen. They took it from where it came from. It went downtown because that's where the money was."

A job at the Coronet, a bar in Brooklyn's Bedford-Stuyvesant black ghetto, was the closest Cecil ever came to facing a community audience in the last few years. The Coronet is a hip, white-owned bar frequented by the members of a large Brooklyn-based community of jazz musicians, some of them involved in the new music. Two of the saints of the Coronet are John Coltrane and Jackie McLean. It would seem a most receptive place for Cecil's music to be exposed to a predominantly black audience, but in 1962, when he played there, the audience was anything but receptive. The competitiveness between musicians who are not involved in the new music with those who are had a good deal to do with the reception. Even though Coltrane and Jackie McLean are the two leaders of the new musical direction of the Coronet, the old-style funk of the 1950's still dominates it. The Coronet funk players had taken on some of the more progressive aspects of the music of Coltrane and others, but they had not gone so far as to absorb the new developments of musicians such as Cecil Taylor. As this job was the first time Cecil had performed in a ghetto since he reached musical maturity, the reaction must be noted here. Sonny Murray describes the scene: "It was sort of a one-sided set-up, that's all I could say. It seems that the club owner decided to hang a number of Cecil's [record] jackets on his walls, and he wanted Cecil to play there because he had heard his records and the records had made a large reputation for Cecil. When the group got there, we found he had left a Negro manager in charge who seemed to feel that this music was not good enough for the Coronet. After the first set, he contacted Cecil and told him that he was fired. He just said, 'We don't want this music in here, you're fired.'

"Cecil was very hurt, very dragged. The people were digging it, they dug Henry [Grimes, the bassist], they dug me. They dug Cecil. It was the power in the music that they really dug. Cecil was very hurt, I could sense that. He bit his lip like he always does and he went back upstairs. I said, 'Well, dig it, Cecil, they've insulted you and me and the rest of the group so let's get our hats.' Cecil said, 'Sonny, please let's just finish it.' I said, 'Why should we finish it, they've insulted us, they don't want us here.' Cecil convinced me to stay, and when I went downstairs to go back on my drums one of the manager's friends told me, 'Man, I don't want to hear you play no more drums.' I said, 'Get out of here and leave me alone. You haven't even listened to what I'm playing, so like you've got no reason to be pissed with me but I have a lot of reasons to be pissed with you.' Anyway, he pulled out a very large switchblade and said, 'You see this?' I took my drum set and closed it up, it's about six pounds and a very strong steel, and I said, 'Well, you see this? Now I will bust your head wide open, brother.' But he was cooled out because his old lady came over and said, 'Come on, you both be cool.'

"But you see, man, that next night Jackie McLean was hit in the mouth by someone from the same crowd. Because he had been sitting there digging Cecil, and when he went up to play the next night he tried to play something experimental with Tony Williams and they came up and hit him in the mouth, and Jackie was supposed to be straight in that bar. This was the whole exhibition at the Coronet, and all it was, was about the bartender trying to protect his friends."

Cecil says: "My experience up in Brooklyn, in a ghetto community, was not the result of the fact that the music wasn't getting to them, but that the night manager was a black man who had an interest in keeping the music from getting to the community because he was committed to a certain camp in the community. The bartender, you know how bartenders are, he worked on those people. Man, I could feel what was going on because like the audience will always give it back to you. I could sense that there was an exchange happening, and since I had people at the bar I was also hip to what the bartender was doing. I feel that if there could have been a minimum of outside interference, if there can be some way by which those people could have gotten into the place and sat down among circumstances in which communication would have been possible, then they couldn't have denied the music. The notes that we play are old music, man. It's old in the sense that there's nothing new there. When you play with authority then that's what the music is about, like ooooooh baby, and sing it. You've got to hear it and those people will hear it too, if all that shit is reduced."

It must be emphasized that the Coronet is not strictly a community bar, but is a kind of expatriate musicians' bar where jobs are jealously guarded, and the vested interests in the kind of music that is played at the Coronet are the factors that determine just what kind of reception a particular group will get. The difference between a Cecil Taylor and a John Coltrane or a Jackie McLean in the eyes of the Coronet audience is that Coltrane and McLean "paid their dues"—they have worked their way up through the established groups, like Miles Davis, Art Blakey, and Dizzy Gillespie, which, in the eyes of much of the jazz community, is prerequisite to achieving the kind of notoriety that Cecil Taylor had already achieved. The reaction, then, was as much a matter of economic competition as of musical taste.

Cecil's status as an outsider in the community of jazz musicians was best proven by the Coronet incident. Alienated from both the white and black communities, and having bound himself up with the kind of economics that dominate most of the arts, there is little that the jazz musician can do about his predicament. That he, as a performing artist, is confronted with a labor predicament in the pursuit of his art, that he even, as Archie Shepp says, "transmits a class experience," only complicates matters. And there is little prospect that the jazz bars will proliferate to the point that they may hire a sufficient number of jazz musicians to relieve the situation. Certainly they will be unable to hire enough musicians to create a climate and an environment in which the musicians can be free to develop their music to its fullest potential.

It is promising that the audience has chosen in a sense to organize itself so that the Cecil Taylors may have a place to play. LeRoi Jones's Black Arts group, for one, has done much to present the new music to the Harlem community. However, because of the high cost of providing live entertainment in bars, along with the other reasons that make it economically unfeasible for the bar owners to fill their traditional roles in the fostering of jazz, this does not promise much in the way of creating areas of work in the Negro community. Nor do such nonprofit groups as the Gotham Jazz Society, the Friends of Jazz, and the now-defunct Jazz Unlimited promise more than occasional work. Given this kind of total displacement from the black community, it seems that the Cecil Taylors will have to mine the affluent sections of American cities—where they probably will find only frustration and even further alienation.

For Cecil there are two markets immediately available that would seem to be now his greatest hope. The first is Europe. Buell Neidlinger, Cecil's bassist for many years, says: "He's expressed to me the feeling that in Europe it's possible, but that in America it's not. Hopefully he'll go to Europe with a group and keep them working for a long time. I think that that will be the solution to much of this thing. The American situation for jazz is the most miserable that I have ever seen. And it's not getting any better. Now that I don't make my living from it anymore, I can see it quite objectively, and I think it's getting worse. But in Europe perhaps it will be better. I understand that they like the new jazz in the Scandinavian countries especially, and also in Germany, France, and Italy now that the die-hard moldy figs who demanded Sidney Bechet and Louis Armstrong for so many years are dying out and the younger generation is coming along and is more interested in what happened since Miles Davis. So Cecil may have a chance there. He says he likes the pianos; he says that even though the businessmen there are crooks too, at least they are sophisticated crooks and it's easier to deal with them. But I think that the American situation is impossible."

Cecil's other hope would seem to be the universities. Buell Neidlinger, again: "The concerts in colleges and universities would be a marvelous outlet for him. Somebody should try to work along these lines for him. He can talk about his music; he is intellectually solid and revealing. Also his music is unique, very strong and dynamic, and for a one-evening presentation in a university it could be quite enthralling. I think Cecil Taylor is potentially the most important musician in the Western World. I am convinced of this. And I'm basing this on my experience with some of the very best of the new composers and the new orchestras as well as many of the better men in the jazz industry. And Cecil has it, to my mind, clearly above all of them. So that if he developed a reputation along those lines as a speaker as well as player, explaining his music to college audiences, I'm sure that he would have no trouble keeping himself and the group very busy.

"I found it with my own experience this year in America that there are about eleven hundred colleges and universities that do present concert series of various types rather than the usual string quartets, piano recitals, vocal recitals style. They're presenting [classical Indian sitarist] Ravi Shankar and John Lewis, and some strange and very different varieties of groups. The avant-garde is growing by leaps and bounds in the universities. The MENC, the Music Educators National Convention, which is all the public school music teachers, have now adopted the avant-garde. At their most recent convention they presented a concert by our Buffalo group which was very well attended, and they are now publishing so-called avant-garde music, although, of course, what they're publishing is now about thirty years old. But to them it is really something, because they're used to very old-fashioned music. I think Cecil could capitalize on that in America, but I think really that his market is in Europe right now."

Cecil's own description of his European tour does not indicate a substantially more promising scene for him than the one he is trying to escape or improve on in America. On the positive side, he said: "The ideal thing would be to have the kind of situation that you do have in Europe. In some of those small towns you have small concert halls or auditoriums that are acoustically perfect. You have instruments, I'm talking about pianos, that are excellent. You have an audience that comes there prepared to be moved. That's it. That's what you pay for. What more could you want than that? But when you work in New York, the Mafia man pays you your money. In Europe you don't have to deal with the Mafia."*

But when he talks about his dealings with European club owners, booking agents, and the like, his description of them sounds very much like home: "Now you talk about some gangsters, those cats over there, now they do a lot of the same things, but they do it in a lot smoother way."

On the whole, though, he found the humiliation less severe and the opportunities for playing before a large audience much broader. The communications media were more open to his music than they ever were in America, where he has made but two brief television appearances, both on an educational network.

Jimmy Lyons and Sonny Murray, who went to Europe with Cecil, felt that it was the best thing that ever happened to the group. They worked consistently for six months and were thereby able to carry the music into areas they had not been able to explore before because the opportunities to

* It is a well-known fact that many of the bars in New York City are Mafia-owned, and I have heard reasonably reliable reports about Mafia ownership of some of the city's most prosperous nightclubs and discothèques. However, in all fairness, I cannot say that I know definitely that any jazz clubs are Mafia-owned even though I have often heard this from jazz musicians. Probably Cecil has good reason to say this. I cannot confirm it.

perform had been so limited. There had never been so much regular work in the United States.

Still, neither the universities nor Europe can solve the basic dilemma with which Cecil, like every serious black musician, is now faced: how to maintain those roots within the community that fructify and justify the music. The racial awareness that the Negro is expressing now is certainly not lost on the jazz musician. The problem, then, is how to live in this society that seems to despise both a black man and an artist, and stay the same man all day long. Cecil says: "That's what the Jazz Composers' Guild was all about. We had hoped to get together and to try to make conditions that were more the way we felt would benefit the musicians and, like, not necessarily the gangsters that we usually have to deal with."

In brief, the history of the Jazz Composers' Guild is this. In the fall of 1964, a group of young jazz musicians, led by trumpeter-composer Bill Dixon, organized a series of concerts which they called the October Revolution in Jazz. The concerts were immensely successful musically, and extremely well attended. Taylor and Bill Dixon reviewed the success of the October Revolution in Jazz, and thought that perhaps they could go considerably further in ameliorating the musicians' conditions. Since the union had proved itself totally inadequate for the jazz musician's purposes and uninterested in his needs, they would organize a guild.* They

---

* Most jazz musicians feel that the union, Local 802 of the American Federation of Musicians, is uninterested in them except at dues-paying time, though they must belong in order to work. For example, a strong and committed union could lobby for repeal of the law requiring a police-issued card for work in cabarets in New York City. This is a discriminatory law that keeps addicts and ex-addicts who are musicians out of work.

would produce their own concerts on a regular basis, thereby
paying the musicians equitably and providing funds for
Guild activities. Contracts for nightclub and concert work
produced by people other than the Guild would have to
be negotiated with the Guild and not with individual musicians, thereby assuring the musicians of legal counsel and
prohibiting exploitative contractual deals with club owners
and producers. The same applied to recording contracts, so
that a given company could pay, say, $75,000 to the entire
Guild for recording rights (actually a saving in terms of all
that the company would be getting). This $75,000 would go
for a building for the Guild, which could then produce its
own concerts on its own premises, establish workshops and
schools, offices and practice rooms. Furthermore, the Guild
would be able to provide legal assistance and to check the
books at the record companies to make sure that royalties
were paid as they should be, and could ascertain that records
were produced at the highest artistic level. If the Guild was
successful, then those jazz musicians who had already
achieved commercial security would be willing to come in.
It would not be practical to ask them to join before the organization was strong.

The idea was a good one, but its execution encountered
many of the same problems that could be expected from
members of a group who are accustomed to taking whatever they can get, accustomed to hustling for every dime
and every job. This was complicated further by racial division within the group. The Guild was comprised of several
highly developed sensitivities, and meetings soon turned into
fights, as there were very real conflicts of interest and of
personality. While it lasted, the Guild's members included
Sun Ra, Archie Shepp, Cecil Taylor, Bill Dixon, Paul and

Carla Bley, Mike Mantler, Burton Greene, and many others,* but after a few artistically successful concerts, it disintegrated over personality differences.

Cecil confirms the racial tension that existed within the Jazz Composers' Guild but also points to a lot of scabbing on the part of its musicians, both white and black, as another main cause for its disintegration. Both Cecil Taylor and Bill Dixon look back on the Jazz Composers' Guild as a good try which probably was bound to fail in its first attempt, but which can succeed in the future if certain mistakes can be avoided and if there is a greater degree of commitment to the idea on the part of the musicians involved. Such organizations, along with the other nonprofit organizations that some listeners are forming, point to some improvement in the jazz condition, but one cannot say with any certainty that such improvements will be good enough. Reviewing the situation, there is little cause for hope.

CECIL TAYLOR AND "SERIOUS" MUSIC

In the liner notes of his *Looking Ahead* (Contemporary) record Taylor said: "Everything I've lived, I am. I am not afraid of European influences. The point is to use them—as Ellington did—as part of my life as an American Negro. Some people say I'm atonal. It depends, for one thing, on

* Sun Ra is a pianist, composer, and orchestra leader who has been working with new forms of jazz for several years. Archie Shepp is a highly articulate tenor saxophonist who has a strong sense of social consciousness, and has had a play, *The Communist*, produced by a theater workshop group. Bill Dixon is the trumpeter-composer who was chiefly responsible for the organization of the Guild. The Bleys are Canadian; both play piano and compose. Mike Mantler is a trumpeter-composer who worked briefly with Cecil Taylor. Burton Greene plays piano and composes.

your definition of the term. . . . I have been atonal in live performances. . . . Basically, it's not important whether a certain chord happens to fit some student's definition of atonality. A man like [Thelonious] Monk is concerned with growing and enriching his musical conception, and what he does comes as a living idea out of his life's experience, not from a theory. It may or may not turn out to be atonal."

There is implicit here a seminationalistic jealousy about his cultural origins which is more or less typical of Cecil Taylor and his contemporaries. He is not ashamed of his conservatory background. (Cecil told Joe Goldberg: "I like hell am [conservatory trained]. If my musical training stopped when I left the conservatory, you wouldn't be talking to me now.") But he does not want his music to be considered as much a product of Europe as of Harlem. He wishes people would listen to the essentially blues content of his music instead of to whatever forms and devices he may have brought over from the conservatory.

Cecil believes that his problem is to utilize "the energies of the European composers, their technique, consciously, and blend this with the traditional music of the American Negro, and to create a new energy. And was it unique? No. Historically not. This is what has always happened. Ellington did it."

Bob Levin quotes Cecil in his notes to the *Hard Driving Jazz* record as saying: "The object of any jazz musician who has had [my] background is to bring it to jazz—combine it with jazz and see what happens. My particular field is jazz and therefore it will eventually become a complete jazz expression. I think it is right for any would-be artist to try and get material from as many places as possible."

Then, somewhat contrarily: "Bartók showed me what you can do with folk material."

It is not surprising that the critics, many of whom have been searching for generations for the missing link between Afro-American jazz and the great body of Western music, have emphasized these influences in writing about Taylor's music. And this is precisely the kind of criticism that incenses Cecil Taylor, because it draws the reader's attention to an aspect of his music that Taylor considers neither minor nor dominant: "I play an extension of period music—Ellington and Monk. Third Stream [the synthesis of jazz and contemporary 'classical' music] is George Gershwin and Ferde Grofé." He has always insisted that his music be taken as a totality, and this insistence has often caught critics who thought they were flattering him off guard. Taylor's reaction to the first important essay ever written about his music has been the subject of discussion among critics for years. The writer was Gunther Schuller, a prominent composer-conductor. He was reviewing Cecil's first two records, *Jazz Advance* (Transition) and *The Cecil Taylor Quartet at Newport* (Verve), in the January, 1959 issue of the now-defunct magazine *The Jazz Review*.

Schuller began his essay with a historical survey of the progressive destruction of the "tonal center" in Western music from the Middle Ages through Schoenberg, Scriabin, Stravinsky, Debussy, Milhaud, Berg, and Webern until music crossed "the borderline into the realm of atonality." Schuller saw, but did not describe, "a course virtually parallel" in the history of jazz until "a small minority of jazz composer-performers are working primarily with the outer reaches of tonality, and have reached that borderline where their music often spills over into areas so removed from any center of tonal gravity, that it can be thought of as 'atonal.' Foremost among these is Cecil Taylor. . . ."

Cecil views this emphasis on tonality or the lack of it

as quite beside the point of his music, but to him the most offensive section of the essay, which was designed not only to compliment him as a musician but also to establish him as an innovator with world-shaking promise, read: "One gets the impression that Taylor is sitting at the piano, *objectively* [italics Schuller's] performing a function to which he was committed, and that in a rather nonparticipating manner he trots out a collection of ideas which, though original and varied enough, have no artistic *raison d'être*. One does not feel the burning necessity that what he says had to be said. Especially on the blues, one has the impression that Taylor lets us in on the workings of his mind, but not his soul. . . ."

This last quotation refers to Cecil's first recording, *Jazz Advance*. Schuller makes a point of stating that this kind of cold musical intellectualizing had not been his usual experience with Cecil Taylor. But, aside from the fact that the Transition date was recorded under unusually cold circumstances, Schuller had unwittingly exposed a particularly sensitive nerve and ground a lighted cigarette in it. He had suggested that the importance, even the validity, of Taylor's music was more technical than soulful, that the music should be approached through its (tonal) form rather than through its (blues) content. To Taylor this was like giving the tractor more credit for the crop than the earth; and anyway the problem of resolving the twentieth-century classical innovations in tonality is more Schuller's concern as an essentially classical composer than Taylor's, as Taylor considers himself a blues improviser.

Cecil's general contempt for critics is now well known. In a 1963 article in the *Village Voice* he wrote: "Critics are sustained by our vitality. From afar, the uninformed egos ever growing arbitrarily attempt to give absolutes."

And Taylor's attitude toward those critics who have

emphasized the classical aspects of his music is well stated in this quotation from Joe Goldberg's *Jazz Masters of the Fifties:* "Now there's one thing that has to be said about critics. Certainly they did attempt to raise the level of writing about jazz. And my appeal to certain of these people I can understand. But it's also like being grateful for small favors. And most of their information was inaccurate. The trouble was they couldn't hear. It was certainly valid for them to say 'I heard such-and-such a composer,' and perhaps so, but what I also heard, and what was also there, were jazz personalities and jazz musicians which they didn't bother to identify because their reference eluded that. Like Horace Silver, like Duke Ellington, like Milt Jackson, like Miles Davis, all that was there."

This not too oblique reference to Schuller's essay is all there is on record to indicate Cecil's reaction to that essay, and when asked, he does not choose to be specific about it. He does describe the confrontation that came at a forum sponsored in 1959 by the United Nations Jazz Society, organized by trumpeter Bill Dixon. Participating from the stage and audience were many of the most advanced minds in the performing and critical jazz establishments, among them Martin Williams, John Lewis, Jimmy Giuffre, and George Russell. Cecil used that occasion to jump on a statement that Schuller had made in another issue of the *Jazz Review.* Cecil recalls: "Schuller had made a remark that it would never occur to Monk to practice and thereby change his technique to improve his music. I asked them, 'Would it ever occur to Horowitz to practice to change *his* technique?' I said, 'Monk can do things that Horowitz can't, and that's where the validity of Monk's music is, in his technique.' I told them that the Schullers wanted to change jazz to fit their own needs; that, essentially, they couldn't recognize the tradition that came from a black subculture as being valid in the face of European culture."

The meaning of technique in jazz as opposed to technique in classical music is a matter of profound concern with Cecil and will receive a good deal of space later. The point here is that it was the razor he used to cut all ties to an avant-garde group of critics—soon to become an establishment itself—that up until then was only too glad to have him. Cecil felt that they needed him more than he needed them. Moreover, Taylor's personality is even more privately self-critical than most artists', and at that stage of his development he must have been acutely aware of those European elements that the critics were happy to unearth in his music. It was he who had digested Europe, and he knew that Europe had not completely settled in his Negro stomach. It was a problem he would have preferred to work out without having the tone rows counted over his shoulder. His feeling, as stated above, is that the artist's work is subject to the interests of the professional audience, but that that audience is similarly susceptible to denunciation by the artist.

Because Cecil Taylor considers extensive discussion of classical influence on his music irrelevant, the best source on that question is Cecil's bassist from 1956–1961, Buell Neidlinger. Buell studied cello from the age of six until he entered Yale, when he started playing bass with a revivalist Dixieland group. When his wife died in September, 1955, Buell came to New York and played at all the Dixieland places with such musicians as Pee Wee Russell, Max Kaminsky, Trummy Young, and Wild Bill Davison. He met the legendary Herbie Nichols, the great modern pianist who had to play Dixieland music for a living. He also met Steve Lacy, a soprano saxophonist who was at the time studying with Cecil Taylor. How they came to form a group will be described later. Suffice it to say here that Neidlinger considers his entrance into Cecil Taylor's group the beginning of his serious musical education, and that he has experienced nothing in his tenure with Houston Symphony Orchestra director Sir John Barbirolli, or with Lukas Foss at the University of Buffalo, that is at all comparable to what Cecil showed him about the possibilities of music.

Buell says: "You asked me about certain references to so-called classical composers when critics have discussed Cecil's work. I'm not too sure whether this is a conscious derivation on Cecil's part or just an unconscious one. It's very hard to say, but I am convinced that there's been an unconscious absorption: that he hasn't sat down with, for instance, scores of Stravinsky and made paraphrases of them or taken certain bars out of Bartók's music and paraphrased them, or used the effects that were in those bars, orchestrated them differently for jazz grouping and used them, though he is certainly capable of doing this. I'm sure this is not what happened; I'm sure his absorption has been unconscious, and total.

"I know that he has a lot of scores, and even more records, of so-called classical music, and that he has been listening to classical music since his youth. He also studied privately from a classical musician when he was a kid, and at the New York College of Music and at the New England Conservatory, where you're definitely exposed to that kind of music. But a lot of critics felt that he has been trying to copy these musics, and I know that isn't true. Cecil is the first cat who has used these systems, or whatever you want to call them, and made them work for jazz, which makes me think that all his music is really very personal, and any kind of allusion to classical music is strictly accidental or subconscious.

"It was a funny thing, when I went up to Buffalo this year, many of the people up there were asking me all about Cecil, but when I came back, Cecil was very anxious for me to tell him how these composers were shaping their music, 'ordering' it, he calls it. He wanted to know the systems and the formats they use. Sooner or later we'll have a conversation about it and I'll tell him what I know."

The contemporary American composer John Cage recently criticized modern jazz for using regular intervals and for being based too much on the emotions. When asked to comment on this, Cecil said: "He doesn't have the right to make any comment about jazz, nor would Stravinsky have any right to make evaluations about jazz, because they don't know the tradition that jazz came out of. I've spent years in school learning about European music and its traditions, but these cats don't know a thing about Harlem except that it's there. Right away, when they talk about music they talk in terms of what music is to them. They never subject themselves to, like, what are Louis Armstrong's criteria for beauty, and until they do that, then I'm not interested in what they have to say. Because they simply don't recognize the criteria."

This attitude has gotten Cecil into innumerable arguments with some of the leading composers of electronic, graph, and chance compositions, and these arguments have generally started from particulars of composition and wandered into cultural values. He considers much of the new European music a joke:

"Last summer [1964] I went over to the Judson Church to hear the [Karlheinz Stockhausen work] *Zeitmesse,* and there were all the Storm Troopers, shuttling everybody around and trying to look like they were going to punch somebody in the mouth if they didn't love the music. It was too funny. I tried not to, but I laughed. Everybody got so salty that I laughed again. It's very funny how this German cat comes over here and tells the Americans, who have all the mechanical tools to do everything beyond them, what's happening. And like they [the Americans] go for it.

"Stockhausen had those cats improvising to get to what he called 'realization.' What does that mean? Like, those cats showed me the scores, because they know I don't like them. See that death wish again? Because they knew what I was going to say. They showed me the scores, and the scores said this: 'We are very pretty. Look how pretty we are.' And they are very pretty, all of them. It's like a painting. I can show you the scores, the Stockhausen there, a percussion score with boxes, written in three languages, with English on the last page, of course. They're only approximations, like guides to tell you what to do with your potential. In a sense, any-body can read that and, in terms of his potential, make a thing.

"Jazz improvisation comes out of a human approach. Stockhausen's essentially like a meticulous, slow worker who knows each instrument, but he doesn't create any music. He never has created any music. He's created, like, colors, but any music that's resulted from his creation has been acci-dental; not even incidental, but accidental."

Conceptually, Cecil sees the new concrete approach to be a treadmill, a frantic attempt to break as many chains to traditional ways of making things as modern technology is doing. The result in both instances, to Taylor, is the destruc-tion of the human element: "Stockhausen's menagerie of effects was, when they were translated, just musical sounds, the way the notes that you read from a Bach thing are musical sounds. In jazz, the cats don't waste their visual energy. They don't divide themselves, and they should divide themselves even less. You look at the instrument and you spend your energy creating sound with the instrument. The point is that the more diverse symbols take away from the actual doing.

"David Tudor is supposed to be the great pianist of the modern Western music because he's so detached. You're damned right he's detached. He's so detached he ain't even there. Like, he would never get emotionally involved in it; and dig, that's the word, they don't *want* to get emotionally involved with music. It's a theory, it's a mental exercise in which the body is there as an attribute to complement that exercise. The body is in no way supposed to get involved in it.

"It's like this painter. I said, 'Like that painting of yours could have been done by a machine,' and he said, 'Well, the human body is just a machine.' The most exciting level of creativity as expressed to me by these people is like that of a machine. For them, the ultimate in kicks is to be a machine."

Yet Cecil Taylor has no compunction about transferring to jazz any innovations that might be useful. He opened his section of a December, 1963 Jazz Composers' Guild Concert at New York's Judson Hall with an improvisation for tuned piano. Strumming tuned piano strings is a device rarely used in jazz, and it is obvious that all those blues chords and chord changes, rhythms and melodies that have been the definitive substance of jazz could not be played in any recognizable way on the inside of a tuned piano. But the piece was well received by the jazz-oriented audience, and Cecil, who feels that he has only one music, whether it is played inside or outside the piano, and who regards himself as nothing but a jazz musician, did not feel that he had compromised himself in the least. Buell Neidlinger described the performance: "I don't find any of the sounds Cecil makes on the inside of the piano at all similar to John Cage or Christian Wolff or Stockhausen or Kagel. I know he's heard all that music, but the implements that he uses to play the inside of the piano are nothing like the ones that they use. For instance, he uses bed springs, steel mesh cloth, things that he lives around. And like those cats are using rubber erasers, corks, and felt mallets. Cecil's is a much more metallic sound, very brilliant, but the Western cats soften the piano down.

"In the Judson performance I played the sustaining pedal and the keyboard and Cecil played the inside of the piano. It was fabulously successful, but it was entirely improvised on the spur of the moment—there was absolutely no rehearsal of that at all. On that tune there was just the drums and myself, and I was able to reach under the piano with my left foot and play the bass at the same time.

"Cecil designed the lighting himself. He had the guy move the rheostats up and down to have a specific kind of lighting effect.

"Now I know, as I describe it, this sounds a lot like contemporary European music. But really, these effects—the lighting and the playing inside the piano, etcetera—as used by the European and American composers, have become so overused and jaded. Cecil's didn't remind me at all of what any of those guys are doing. It's hard to say why it didn't. You'd think it would, but it didn't. Maybe it's because, even though I hadn't played with Cecil in three years I've spent so much time with his music that I could play it with him in an entirely new format."

Cecil Taylor's position is that, if you can evaluate jazz in classical terms, you can evaluate classical music in jazz terms: "Thelonious Monk and Charlie Parker wrote leads that have all the energy and all the rhythmic qualities of a symphony in twelve measures. They say I follow Europe, but everybody who's hip knows that the Europeans are looking, really, at jazz. The long form is exhausted. Nobody writes long-form music anymore. It's nineteenth century. The sonata is out, old-fashioned. That's what Webern is about. So, it means that what they're trying to get to is the kernel, the short musical statement. When they come to the point where everything happens, where the development, the climax is, that's good. Why not just give me that? That's music; that should stand by itself."

Cecil considers his music "constructivist," a concept he recognized first in Dave Brubeck's early music, but which he has developed through several steps simply by the abundance of the materials he uses and by the placement of those materials in all the voices of his group. Thus: "The emphasis in each piece is on building a whole, totally integrated structure. In doing this, we try to carry on—in ensemble as well as solo sections—the mood of a jazz soloist. I mean that principle of kinetic improvisation that keeps a jazz solo building. What makes jazz unique is the compression of that energy into a short period of time, and that, in turn, is a reflection of what the machine has done to our lives in metropolitan areas in America."

Or: "Music is the organization of sound existing in time, its dimensions hanging in space. The problem was reorganization of ingredients to discover surprise. Harmonic changes provided yesterday's dynamism. Additive technique, extended phrases, slowing down of harmonic motion, diads, clusters replace chords built on thirds. Rhythmic possibilities are expanded, and knowledge of given time is understood. And the ecstatic compression of time's energy produces twelve, sixteen, and thirty-two measures—complete sketches, improvisation, content, and shape becoming one."

By Cecil's definition, however, the master constructivist would have to be Ellington: "Of course I know that the key to European music is construction, like that's what you listen to more than anything else in European music—form, shape. But for me, I have to take into account the literature of jazz music as I've heard it . . . the great cats. Ellington is one. In that period—'39, '40, '41, and '42—he did more in utilizing the different instruments in his band in more different ways than anyone. He could play a blues, but man, the way the thing was laid out it transcended the single idea of the blues. I'm still trying to come to grips with that, you know. I'm still trying to come to grips with every instrument I use, to the extent that he used his, in terms of, like, color and particularly technique. The cats have more technique now. Like I want to get colors out of sound the way Ellington did."

Cecil Taylor's keyboard technique has never been questioned. By any standard of facility he is easily the most capable of the major jazz pianists. He is as fast as Tatum, as strong as Powell, as subtle as Lewis; and he is likely to be all these things in any one given piece. He is able to play simultaneous arpeggios with both hands at the most rapid tempi, or he can throw out overwhelming complexes of chords from both ends of the piano.

There is a power and weight to Cecil's playing, a heavy energy that pervades the room while he plays. No one, not even the most negative of his critics, ever leaves a Cecil Taylor performance unimpressed with the things he can do on the piano; critic Zita Carno, for one, thought that Taylor does so much that it makes him a bad, overly busy, accompanist. Other critics have felt that Taylor's technique runs away with him, and that he should be more restrained, should edit his playing more. Those listeners who have been consistently moved by the sheer density of Cecil's playing swear by his technique as inseparable from the divers materials and effects that are the body of his playing.

Cecil makes no such separation: "I've had great arguments lately with cats who wish to make all kinds of separation between form, content, and technique, but I tell them that technique isn't anything divorced from the end product. It doesn't matter where your technique comes from, or whether it's 'correct' or not. It will be correct if your music is strong."

For Cecil, the question of technique is more philosophical than practical. He does not worry about his own skill at any kind of piano playing: "I know some of the literature of classical piano. I've prepared it to the satisfaction of some people who were specialists in that. I could play Bach fugues and so could many a jazz pianist if they were interested. But they're not interested, they're just not interested."

From this point of view, the statement quoted earlier that "Monk can do things Horowitz can't, and that's where the validity of Monk's music is, in his technique" logically follows. The process of performing jazz is as different from the process of performing classical music as the end products of those processes. He finds it no disadvantage that Ornette Coleman taught himself violin in a manner that would never satisfy a competent violin teacher: "Cats said to me, 'Well, you know Ornette really doesn't know much about the violin.' I said, 'What do you mean?' 'Well, he couldn't play like Heifetz!' We got back into that thing I thought I'd left at the U.N. back in 1958. Like, in spite of Heifetz' great technique, he has never come up with a sound like Ornette. He has never played the music that Ornette plays on the violin. I've heard Jose Iturbi play boogie-woogie; who plays boogie better than Pete Johnson? If, like, the doing is an expression of this hidden concept, technique, and if you admit that Pete Johnson plays boogie-woogie better, doesn't it mean that in this area, which is a colored area, you have to grant that he's a superior technician?

"Interestingly, I've had this argument with a colored guy who frequents one of those West Village bars with his little beard, and he got enraged. I said, 'Well, man, what you're really trying to tell me is that as a Negro you feel inferior, and because you feel it, like, you are. So goodbye.'"

Taylor makes an interesting analogy between technique and language: "In returning to this concept of what technique is, like, I've talked to these British intellectuals, and they can tell you about Shakespeare, man. They can tell you about how expressive Shakespeare's language was, and their own language, I listened to their syntax, it was clear and lucid, and so very proper. But they don't seem to understand that there's another English language, American, which has nothing to do with the King's English. Then when you get down to the language, the American English language, of Harlem, then that's something else again. Like, whose language is correct when an Englishman talks to a cat from 125th Street? And if they can't understand each other, is the Englishman superior?

"But when you start talking to the people about what music is about, why, just what is it that makes Horowitz' touch superior, then I don't know on the basis of what presumption they're going to talk about Monk's limited technique. It always comes out to, 'Well, we've got this tradition,' or some shit like that. I have a tradition, and my tradition informs me the way that theirs informs them, perhaps. I don't have the academies to forward my tradition, but I do have that small department that Bud Powell was teaching. And that was long enough ago, the way the twentieth century moves, to make a tradition. Why isn't that a valid way of doing it, too?"

Cecil actually found the textbook mechanics disadvantageous: "I'm talking about the physicality of it. Take Bud and Tatum. They had fantastic technique—you cannot deny that these cats had phenomenal ability to play the instrument. Tatum played the piano with his fingers outstretched like this. However, I was taught to play the piano like this [hands cupped], and with infinite variations of curved fingers kind of stuff."

It was, then, necessary for Taylor to unlearn a good deal of what he had been taught in the conservatory: "When I came out of school, the first thing that I did was to walk down 125th Street and listen to what was happening. And it took me maybe a month before I started digging. That was the beginning of, like, the other education. I mean the participation in, and the doing of, the thing."

"The doing of the thing" involves the total involvement of mind and body. Cecil sees a kind of dance to playing jazz piano ("I try to imitate on the piano the leaps in space a dancer makes") and, apart from his interest in all forms of dance, he takes cognizance of the fact that, historically, jazz had been until the 1940's essentially a dance music. He sees this dance tradition as kinetic impetus for the black musician, and its absence as a retarding factor for the white jazz musician. It is an essential of jazz technique: "Like, the physicality . . . you notice the cats who really play, like Horace Silver. Horace has a certain kind of physical movement, a certain way he attacks the piano. If you notice Daddy Ellington, when he plays you'll see that he has a certain thing that he does with his foot, and that foot action is as much a part of what's happening with the keyboard as his hands. It's a part of his technique.

"I saw this white British singer, Petula Clark, on television and she was singing her tune "Downtown," the tune she made it on. Like, it got very humorous because she was screaming and she was trying to look composed at the same time. But when [blues singer and dancer] James Brown goes into his thing, he goes; it's like a complete catharsis. He goes. Every fucking thing goes and there ain't no holding back. And it's beautiful. That's the technique of rhythm-and-blues singing, man, and no academy but the genuine tradition of a people can give it to you."

The definition of proper technique in music must then depend on the cultural origins of that music. Kneeling while screaming and ripping off his shirt is not merely a part of James Brown's showmanship, it is an essential of the communication of the highly emotional songs that James Brown sings, and if he moves the audience, that technique is sound.

Taylor has found that even the idea of written composition often hampers the communication of ideas among the musicians. The tune and the structure must often be transmitted in the same oral fashion that marked the difference between mulatto Jelly Roll Morton and the illiterate black musicians from around the docks. According to Archie Shepp, who played tenor saxophone with Cecil in 1959, "Cecil has returned to natural music. At that point, Cecil stopped writing his music out and started to teach the cats the tunes by ear. He would play the line, and we would repeat it. That way we got a more natural feeling for the tune and we got to understand what Cecil wanted.

"Now a lot of musicians don't want to do that because they have a bourgeois hangup about the whole status of being a competent reader. Richard Davis, who is a good bass player and probably could play with most symphony orchestras if most symphony orchestras hired Negro musicians, had problems playing with Taylor because he didn't trust Taylor's music because it wasn't written. 'Pots' [from Gil Evans' *Into The Hot*, Impulse], which a lot of critics have called a masterpiece of modern jazz composition, was written that way.

"That was the way jazz was written before—by ear; and now Taylor has trouble finding musicians who can meet that challenge. The black man has come full circle."

Jimmy Lyons, who replaced Shepp in Cecil's quintet, had much the same experience: "Sometimes Cecil writes his charts out, sometimes not. I dig it more when he doesn't. I don't know how to say this, but we get like a singing thing going when he teaches us the tunes off the piano. It has to do with the way Cecil accompanies. He has scales, patterns, and tunes that he uses, and the soloist is supposed to use these things. But you can take it out. If you go into your own thing, Cecil will follow you there. But you have to know where the tune is supposed to go, and if you take it there another way than the way Cecil outlined it, then that's cool with Cecil. That's the main thing I've learned with Cecil, the music has to come from within and not from any charts."

Both Shepp and Lyons read music fluently; but for Sonny Murray, an important musician because he is the only drummer who plays completely free time, the charts were a problem: "Cecil has percussion lines written into all of his charts. I had just begun to read music, and it was difficult for me to read Cecil's charts right offhand. It's easier now, but even still I would lose a certain amount of freshness if I played his charts exactly as he writes them.

"When I would come into rehearsals Cecil would say, 'Sonny, if you want to read this, do so, fine.' I would look at it and would see that it was based on so many sixteenths and so many rests, then I would conceive an idea of how to play this. Then I would alternate it according to what I felt my freedom allowed me to do. Later on, when I could read his charts, I still wouldn't play them exactly, I felt that it would be doing his music an injustice to play it exactly, because he could find anybody to do that.

"The first day I started rehearsing with him, I asked him, 'What should I play?' He said, 'Just play.' I said, 'What do you mean? Like a drum solo?' 'No, I mean just let yourself play your drums, but listen too.' And it happened.

"I used this principle throughout all our rehearsals, but I've also accepted the music that he's written. At rehearsals we play at command and will. The music is so exhilarating that if you have any native talent, inspired talent, you just have to create with Cecil. You don't have to wait for Cecil and Cecil doesn't have to wait for you: You play music together."

The implication of all this is that the composition is begun when the musicians are chosen.

Cecil Taylor has a profound concern with both dance and song. Buell Neidlinger said of Cecil's extrapianistic techniques: "We shared an apartment for a while, and I had the opportunity to watch him practice, and his practicing revolves around *solfège* singing. He'll sing a phrase and then he'll harmonize it at the piano and then he'll sing it again, always striving to get the piano to sing, to try and match this feeling of the human production, the voice, in terms of pianistic production so that it gets the same effect. Cecil's trying to get the vocal sound out of the piano, and I think he's achieved it on many occasions. You can almost hear the piano scream or cry. It's worked for him.

"The dance, I think, had its results on his playing because a lot of his playing depends on body motion, especially the fast playing. He does things with a speed that most pianists, if they heard it on a record, would say, 'How does he do that?' It has a lot to do with the rhythmic flailing of his arms or his ability to move his body back and forth like a pendulum from one end of the piano to the other so that he can put his hands in the proper position, and I think his interest in the dance has a lot to do with that.

"He's the first jazz pianist to really exploit the instrument. If you notice, in the symphony orchestras, the piano is listed as a percussive instrument, and Cecil's the first guy to bring that out in jazz."

It is characteristic of the American "establishment's" attitude toward jazz that the Rockefeller Report on the Performing Arts, which attempted to survey the entire situation of the performing artist in America and to propose concrete means of improving the situation, made no mention whatever of jazz. Nor does the recent Federal law to aid the arts make specific provisions for jazz musicians. (There is actually a controversy, as this is being written, about whether jazz qualifies as "folk art" under the terms of the bill!) Cecil Taylor sees the material deprivation of the jazz musician, apart from the almost impossible task of earning a living playing serious jazz, in terms of his own lack: "You see this piano? Not more than half of it works. In a way, this piano is me: it half works; I get to work about half the year. Everything that's wrong with it, I did to it. I knocked those keys out. I can look at that piano and see my work from the last few years. But you know, a cat playing classical music who had come this far would be getting free pianos, because it's good for the industry. Not me, baby. The pianos I get to play on are never more than 60 percent in, have most of the ivory off the keys, and they are never in tune. Now what is that going to do for my music? In Europe, the pianos were much better in the jazz spots, which shows you that they value the music more."

Obviously, the pianist can't care for and tune the instrument he has to perform on, and it is a problem nightclub owners are not particularly sensitive to. Neidlinger said: "I think that one of the most difficult problems that Cecil has to resolve is nightclub pianos. Cecil's a very proud man, and there's so much to his music that sometimes it seems like it would take two pianos to accommodate all that he can do. But when he's asked to get this music out of an instrument that's only half functioning, you know how he must feel.

"So he doesn't want to work in a club unless the piano is tuned every day. That's an economic impossibility for club owners. You know club owners—they couldn't give a damn about how in tune the piano is. Like, there's a piano there, you play it.

"Until an artist has reached a certain stature economically, pulling a large mass audience, such as Erroll Garner or John Lewis, they can't get away with making those demands. On the other hand, it's a practical matter of how can Cecil play the music he plays on half a piano? I've said it again and again. Cecil is one of the most important, if not the most important, musician America has produced since Charlie Parker and those cats—since World War II. But like with Horowitz—after a Horowitz concert they either send the piano back to the factory or sell it to a student. They can't use it again. So with that in mind you can see how ridiculous it is for Cecil to have to endure these bartenders running over every fifteen minutes telling him to take it easy on their beat-up uprights."

Joe Termini, the owner of the Five Spot, confirmed the fear that club owners have when Cecil approaches their pianos: "I had this old upright piano at the old Five Spot, and I wasn't about to buy a new one. So Cecil, he plays very hard, he was playing there, and I asked him to please take it easy on the piano. And just as I asked him, two keys came flying off. Cecil, he's a piano tuner's delight."

For Cecil, however, this is a far more important issue than Joe Termini's upright piano. It involves the whole issue of cultural repression: "The offices of recognition have a yardstick that was set in Europe, which doesn't even acknowledge the idea of American art. The Pulitzer Prize people wanted to give Duke something. Not the whole thing—they didn't give an award for music that year, they didn't find any music that was worth it, which shows you just how they look for 'serious' music. They gave Duke an award for something like years of continuous service. Why not give the music award to Duke Ellington? If they had been giving a truly objective evaluation of the music produced in America year after year, then there are a whole lot of years Papa Ellington would have won. William Schuman and those cats are not like giants of twentieth-century music, but Ellington is, man, Ellington is."

There are no facilities outside of the industry to encourage the growth and development of jazz and jazz musicians. Cecil continues: "Negro music is out of it. Negro dancers are out of it. Negro everything is out of it, and that's where the fight is.

"I've known Negro musicians who've gotten grants, but it's very interesting that no Negro *jazz* musician has ever gotten a grant. If you're a black pianist who wants to learn to play Beethoven, you have a pretty good chance of getting a grant. That's that fucked-up liberal idea of uplifting the black man by destroying his culture. But if you want to enlarge on culture, forget it; your money will have to come from bars and that cutthroat record industry. Sonny Murray should have had a grant two years ago, Milford Graves [a young drummer] should have a grant now. Can you imagine what that would do for the young cats, if they started doing that? But Sonny Murray is an innovator, and he doesn't own his own set of drums. He doesn't have an instrument. I don't have an instrument."

CECIL'S STORY

I was born in Long Island City. I grew up in Corona, Long Island, where there were very few Negroes. A couple of high-yellow families, but the women who lived down the block were more white than anything else. There was even one Negro couple who was passing [for white]. My mother was a housewife and my father a chef-cook. I used to worry a little bit about my father's Southernness, which was my own shortcoming, actually, but since he was working all day his Southernness didn't really matter in terms of my life.

Music to me was in a way holding on to Negro culture, because there wasn't very much of it around. My father had a great store of knowledge about black folklore. He could talk about how it was with the slaves in the 1860's, about the field shouts and hollers, about myths of black people. Also my father was quite knowledgeable about such theatrical personalities as Burt Williams and Florence Mills, and he had seen things like young Satchel Paige pitching and a home run that Josh Gibson hit out of the stadium in Washington, D.C.

He was a product of the development of the city. He came to New York when Delancey Street was the center of the city: around 1910. He worked out in Long Island for a State Senator. He was a house servant and a chef-cook at the Senator's sanatorium for wealthy mental wrecks. And actually it was my father more than the Senator himself who raised the Senator's children.

Sometimes I used to go out to Long Island and eat, since the food was of course a lot better at the Senator's house than at home. As I said, the Senator ran a sanatorium for wealthy mental wrecks. And I remember meeting one of these completely senile Southern gentry who were housed at the sanatorium, and like I put out my hand for the man to shake, the man ignored my hand and said, "Hello boy, how are you?" and kept on talking. And I really used to get dragged at my father for taking such shit off these people. I didn't dig his being a house servant.

I didn't really understand my old man; well, you're from my generation and you know the difference between us and our fathers. Like, they had to be strong men to take what they took. But of course we didn't see it that way. So I feel now that I really didn't understand my father, who was really a lovely cat. He used to tell me to stay cool, not to get excited. He had a way of letting other people display their emotions while keeping control of his own. People used to say to me, "Cecil, you'll never be the gentleman your father was." That's true. My father was quite a gentleman. He came from an agricultural region and he could put his fingers on his Scotch great-grandparents and his Indian mother. I wish I had gotten more from this or about my family; I wish I had pushed them more for information, because it's lost now. Also I wish I had taken down more about all that he knew about the black folklore, because that's lost too; he died in 1961.

My mother's maiden name was Ragland. She had Indian blood too. The Raglands have the flattest noses in the world. My mother's mother was an Indian. Mother played piano, she was the real force in the family. My father was, like, gentle and more collected. Mother spoke French and German, had an interest in the theater; she was the oldest of six girls.

She had been the main impetus for my learning the piano, even though she wouldn't have dug my becoming a jazz musician, obsessed as she was with bourgeois ideas of success. I started taking lessons when I was five. I was fortunate here because the cat across the street was playing tympani with Toscanini, and his wife was a piano teacher. She was quite good and she taught me a lot of things that they were later to give me at the conservatory. Her name was Mrs. Jessey. Later I studied percussion with her husband.

My uncle played the violin but didn't want to commit himself to music. He had a passive personality, liked women and drinking with the fellows, but didn't want to get it done really, like he just didn't dig to get it down in music. But my family, at least on my mother's side, was from Long Branch where the Greers [Sonny Greer was Duke Ellington's drummer for many years] lived, and they were good friends of the Greers. Another uncle played piano and drums, and he took me to hear all the bands. My cousin was supposed to have been the first Negro to play on the radio.

It's good that I studied percussion. See, percussion has always been a big influence on my music, as I think all the critics have pointed out. About this time I started hearing Gene Krupa and Chick Webb. Chick Webb was an especially big influence on me. When I was about six or seven I used to take out the pots and pans and beat on them after digging Webb. Same with Cab Calloway. I'd hear him and start running through the house screaming "hidihidihidihi," shaking my head and trying to make my hair fly, though of course it wouldn't.

A little later I saw Lunceford. That was a really great band which I still dig to listen to. I saw the Goodman band at the Paramount with Hampton, Wilson, and all that crowd. And Tommy Dorsey's band and Artie Shaw and Glen Miller.

I saw Ellington too. Now that's kind of funny because at first when I was a little kid I used to resist Ellington, because Duke was *it* in our family and I always made it a point to disagree with the family. I didn't hear Duke really until the late Forties when I went to hear Lena Horne, who was on the same program with Duke. Now Lena is a great musician. She had Luther Henderson's band behind her and they played only solid music under her. She was the most beautiful woman in show business at the time, and one of the most talented. If she had been white she would have been an incredible movie star and a far more wealthy woman than she is. She could certainly have cut all those white chicks of her generation. Duke had Betty Roche, who can really sing, with him then. That was the band with Barney Bigard, Johnny Hodges, Lawrence Brown, that crew. I heard a lot of Ellington after that. During the war the government had Duke on the radio every Saturday selling war bonds. And hearing him consistently had to get to you. It was like opening a whole new world. Basie's band, too; Basie's band had Illinois Jacquet in it. Now that was a swinging band. Those tunes, "The King" and "Jump," used to move, and that was the time that all the critics were digging Woody Herman.

You know how much dance has influenced my music and my approach to piano playing. About this time I saw the Four Step Brothers doing their leaps and splits, and Baby Laurence, whom I saw later with Charlie Mingus. Now Laurence's coordination of body and feet compares a lot with ballet. I think Baby Laurence and cats like that were our ballet. His foot movements were incredible.

I later on got to work with Bill Bailey, and I also worked with Buck, of Buck and Bubbles. That was in 1954. The Bill Bailey gig was pretty cool because I had not yet developed any kind of style; but by 1954 my style of playing was developed, and Buck hadn't heard me when he called me for the gig, which was in Toronto. He just got my name out of the union book. Well, that was a pretty funny scene. 'Cause Buck was looking, like, for an Art Tatum or an Oscar Peterson at the most modern. He wanted a pianist who could stride. But we went to rehearsals and I had him sweating, man, I really had him sweating. Then, when we were on stage, Buck said to the audience, "Ladies and Gentlemen, I asked for Tatum, I asked for Peterson, and what did I get? Cecil!"

Generally, with the older cats I would figure out what they wanted and give it to them. I played once for some old guy who sounded like a cross between Eldridge and Armstrong, and he was okay. He would say, "Just do what you do." He would sustain a note for like four or five beats and he would expect me to fill it in for him, and that was groovy. It was Lawrence Brown who said to me that a piano player is like a whole orchestra. He has to cover everything and feed everyone. I later on had a great experience working with the Johnny Hodges band, which included Emmett Berry and Lawrence Brown and some tenor player from Philadelphia who might have been John Coltrane. Later on Richie Powell replaced me with that band. It was a good experience for me. It was as close as I ever came to working with the Ellington orchestra.

My mother died when I was, like, thirteen or fourteen. I guess that took something out of me, because after her death I gave up piano and started putting in long hours playing basketball and running track. I was a long-distance runner, I ran the half-mile, the mile, and all that. I was pretty good, and won a few trophies. I don't know why I went back to playing piano, I really can't remember. But I do know that when I was in high school I won a contest on WHN radio with a friend who played drums. A cat named Ostroff heard me on this radio program and called me up to set up an audition with a band he had. He had all these connections for gigs up in the Catskill resorts, you see. Well, I showed for the audition and I found that there were, like, ten pianists there. I cut them all on reading and technique and all that, and I went around on some local gigs with Ostroff. Then one summer Ostroff had this gig for this big hotel in the Catskills, but when the owner of the hotel came down to see the band play its arrangements and saw that Ostroff had hired, like, a Negro musician, he said that he couldn't use Negro musicians in his hotel. Ostroff took the gig anyway and dropped me. That was my first professional experience.

I think that it was 1951 when I went up to Boston. I had relatives in Boston, a cousin that was sort of a brown part of the black-white gentry. That is, they lived in the New England version of a Southern White Christian's manor house. The reigning matriarch in that family was a fierce woman named Blanche, who ran the house. Lunceford's music was big in that house. It was outside the black section. Hell of a big contradiction in that family. They had French Creole background, and they were fiercely anti-white. But then my cousins' two cousins both married Negroes who were whiter than white.

In 1952 I went to the New England Conservatory. I took piano for the first three years along with arranging, harmony, and advanced *solfège*. In school with me were some people who finally made it, like Adele Addison, and

Kenneth Schermerhorn, who now does some pretty anti-septic conducting of Stravinsky at the American Ballet.

I've got to say that I learned more either outside of school or from the nonacademic aspect of school than I did in the classes. The head of the Composition Department was such a bigot that he wouldn't let me into the department. They had one Negro in the Composition Department named Gomez, who was the outstanding student in that department at that time. The Composition Department was the best department in the school, and one of the best among the East Coast schools—that is, Juilliard, Eastman, Curtis, Yale, and Harvard. But that department head, he must have figured that he already had one Negro and that was enough. He couldn't really figure out what we were doing there. Even when he was trying to be nice, he was a racist. I remember once he said to me, "Your music is all right, but it's mood music. That's okay as long as it's not 'Mood Indigo.'" Now that was his idea of a friendly joke, telling me that there was something wrong with "Mood Indigo." That meant to me that I had to be black if for no other reason than that they thought that black was bad.

Anyway, I learned more music from Ellington than I ever learned from the New England Conservatory. Like learning an orchestral approach to the piano from Ellington, like, I could never have gotten that from the Conservatory.

Then there was this old saxophone player at the Conservatory who taught me all the bop changes. His name was Andrew McGhee and he played with Hampton and was recently working with Woody Herman at the Five Spot. He played, like, an extremely fast but dead kind of tenor that was like Sonny Stitt, but even more mechanistic than Stitt's. Andrew pointed out to me the good Boston jazz musicians: Gigi Gryce, Jackie Byard, who was *the* jazz pianist of Boston at the time, Charlie Mariano, Herb Pomeroy, Sam Rivers, and Serge Chaloff. Chaloff was to me the most talented of the white musicians in Boston at this time, but he ruined himself by laying with Herman so long.

So I finally started to go to the clubs to hear the music. In Boston you could walk across the bridge to the other side of town and be in the black ghetto. Of course the better jobs were in the white clubs, but some of the black musicians were equally well known on both sides of the bridge. The good jobs never seemed to fall their way; they invariably lived and worked in the ghetto. The Hi-Hat is the club in which I saw Bird in 1951. It was located in the farthest-out point in the ghetto.

Of course I had heard Bird before on records, but man, like you've really never heard him until you've dug him standing in front of the audience and sweating. That was the real Bird, and I never heard anything like it. I also heard Sarah [Vaughan] for the first time during that period, that was young Sarah, before she adopted all the mannerisms she is known for now. In '51 when she was sitting in with Dizzy in Boston, she was at her best, she broke it all up. She cut Ella Fitzgerald, who was the established singer at the time and was on the same bill.

There was a lot of music going on in my early years in Boston. Like I heard Bud [Powell] at this time, and even though I felt that it was a spiritually different music, I couldn't identify with it. Later on I heard Bud's recording of *Un Poco Loco,* and it completely extinguished the Tristano influence which was strong in me in the early Fifties. I also heard later on a concert in Boston in which Mary Lou Williams was playing the piano, and, like, she was playing like Erroll Garner, but her music had a lot of range. I even dig the sonics that Garner can get from the piano, and Mary Lou put that together too.

A guy that's playing with Woody Herman now, Nat Pierce, had the band, the white band up in Boston at the time that was causing the most talk. Nat plays piano with Woody Herman now, and he made arrangements that seem to me to be a cross between Woody Herman and Stan Kenton.

There were several Negro bands, one led by a cripple trombonist who came from Florida and had all the cats in the bands in Boston at the time. I don't remember his name. I went to several rehearsals of that band, and it was one of the legends that you hear about. You know, the music was right. It was great in terms of the times. A proving ground a lot of cats developed out of.

Joe Gordon was the trumpet power there, and I was at the dance when Charlie Parker and Red Rodney were playing, and I remember Joe walking up to the bandstand and asking Bird if he could play, and Bird said, "Well yes," you know, and gave a mumble. The tune Bird called was in his walkaway tempo, and of course Joe was nervous and wasn't really making it. But Bird looked at him and dug him because he saw that Joe was fighting it. But he also dug that this boy was more than just a local hero, so the next piece he called was at a medium tempo. Of course Joe got into his thing and Bird looked at him amazed and said, "Has Dizzy Gillespie heard you play?" because that's the way Joe was playing, and of course Red Rodney was burnt. That might have been 1950. He was something. He was then what he was when he came to New York in 1952.

I later witnessed a couple of funny scenes with Joe Gordon in Birdland, one with Miles Davis when Miles heard Joe play and then walked off the stand, and Bird ran up to

Miles and grabbed him by the arms and said, "Man, you're Miles Davis," and Miles sort of came back and stood around shuffling his feet, that was funny, you know, you know Miles. Another time Idres Sulieman was playing trumpet, I think that may be more interesting because Idres didn't have the reputation that Miles had, but he was a hard worker and a man who investigated all the possibilities. So that when Joe played his stuff, Idres just stood back and watched him, and then went ahead and played what he played. Very interesting, because the audience responded to Joe Gordon immediately, but I think the musicians who were digging understood the difference between intelligent investigation in an area where many lines are passing through as opposed to the catharsis of music as this develops in a small community. That is, Joe was essentially playing Dizzy Gillespie, while Idres Sulieman was playing Idres Sulieman at this point, which had Gillespie in it, as well as some other trumpet players, but that was still, in its way, perhaps more personal.

Boston was full of musicians at the time. And another who was quite good as a pianist and also one of the leaders is a man named Sam Broadnax. I met him in the basement of a conservatory where a lot of people used to come and play the piano. You see, you had to pay for all your practicing time at the conservatory, and these rooms were the cheapest available because, like, they were right next to the furnace and they had these old upright pianos with wooden doors. Broken glass was all around, and since these were the most uncomfortable rooms, they were never monitored and you could sneak in and practice for free. Also people from outside the conservatory would come in and practice. Sam Broadnax was there one day and playing by himself, and McGhee and I came down to play, and then we overheard him. He had thick harmonic textures, and I had never heard the piano played that way before. Broadnax was really into it, and I learned a lot by listening to him.

Then there was this white cat, Dick Twardzik. He was a leading white exponent of Bud Powell, but I understand his bag included Tristano and Erroll Garner and some others. And when I went back in 1955, he had destroyed some Kenton people by playing like Bud Powell first and getting them all excited and then going into his, at that time, Schoenbergian bag while they were playing Erroll Garner chords. He was like the white pianist power up there.

Herb Pomeroy's band was working at the time at the Stable, which had only been in existence for a little while. But the Stable was a growing concern, and they were open to cats playing.

I remember that this was about the time of the year, during the summer, when they had that festival in the Commons Park, with painting and dance. Martha Graham danced up there. And some abstract expressionists were shown that year. It was that year that jazz was included for the first time. They had Twardzik and Pomeroy's band playing.

After that concert was over we all retired to the Stable thoroughly evil because of the kind of jazz we'd heard, and I decided that I would play. My conception had developed by then, and while I was playing, Twardzik came in, and he sort of did a dance around the edge of the piano. I found out afterward that he thoroughly approved of the goings-on, but he was very upset by it because he couldn't believe it was happening.

I must have been playing something like the Transition record.* I did admire Horace at the time, I still thought of

* The reference is to Taylor's first record, *Jazz Advance*, on the Transition label.

Tristano, but I was really involved with Miles's playing and Milt's playing very much, and Sonny's playing and Monk, of course, and Stravinsky was not as much in my mind but he was still there. I had all those sources I was still drawing from, and of course, Ellington. I never would have thought of playing the piano without thinking it out along Ellington's lines, and that's the base.

When I came [back to Boston] in 1955, there was this other place, which I don't remember the name of, but it was in the Negro neighborhood. This place reminded me of the Paradise in that there were those unsophisticated people, at least they looked unsophisticated. But, like, if my music is sophisticated, then they must have been too, because they gave me one of the best responses that I've ever had. Yeah, I really dug it.

McGhee was mostly instructing me as to who the musicians were and how well they played. I was also digging that people like Gigi Gryce were not working in places that the big-name people from New York, like Bud and Stan Getz and Oscar Peterson, were working at, but these were the cats known to the local musicians. I heard Jackie Byard, for instance; he was playing piano with Serge Chaloff, and doing it in a most discontent way. It was fairly obvious that he was a hell of a piano player who didn't dig the leader he was working with, so he just tossed off things. He was good. I remember being interested in seeing just how much he could do. At that time he was the pianist that the local pride boys used whenever Bud Powell came into town, and he would work opposite Bud. Sam Rivers was the saxophonist up there at that time. I never heard him, but McGhee told me he heard us, you know, that he respected us. A lot of the musicians, I guess, felt that way too. And of course Charlie Mariano was pointed out as the leading white imitator of

Charlie Parker. And Mariano had been taught by Gigi Gryce.

Among the nonmusicians I met during '51 and '52 were Terry Carter and Nat Hentoff. Terry Carter was an actor who was politically involved. I knew him in New York. Carter introduced me to political people like Pete Seeger, and Hentoff had me on his jazz show. Hentoff had a jazz show on WMEX once a week and did a gospel show live once or twice a week. He later on went to Europe on a Guggenheim. I went up to the studio with Carter and played a boogie-woogie duet with him. Hentoff invited me up, and we later established a correspondence.*

It was earlier, in '51–'52 that I became aware of certain contrary ideas in my own playing which had to be resolved. Like, when Brubeck opened in 1951 in New York I was very impressed with the depth and texture of his harmony, which had more notes in it than anyone else's that I had ever heard. It also had a rhythmical movement that I found exciting. I went over and told him what I had heard, and he was amazed that anyone could see what he was doing. Remember, this is Brubeck of the Tentet, when he was still serious. I don't think that that music is important now for what it made, but I still think that it was important then, for the gaps it filled. I was digging Stravinsky, and Brubeck had been studying with Milhaud. But because of my involvement with Stravinsky, and because I knew Milhaud, I could hear what Brubeck was doing, which amazed Brubeck. Brubeck called

---

* Nat Hentoff remembers first meeting Taylor in the Symphony Record Shop, a Boston collector's shop: "Cecil obviously knew a lot about all kinds of music. I later went to a concert of student music and Cecil was very analytical of the music, but in constructive terms. He gave me all kinds of insight, which I used in my own work, in my own approach to music. We talked about jazz, and I remember that Cecil had a very strong sense of tradition, and that he did not feel he had to prove his hipness."

[saxophonist Paul] Desmond over, but Desmond's attitude was standoffish. Reputedly during that show, Dizzy Gillespie had thrown eggs up on the stage. Dizzy was working opposite Brubeck with a band that had Percy Heath, Milt Jackson, and John Lewis. That band of Dizzy's was so much more than Brubeck's band, but of course Brubeck had by then started to cop all the headlines in the magazines.

I found Brubeck's work interesting until I heard Tatum, Horace Silver, and Oscar Peterson within a period of six weeks. Of that crowd, I found Tatum the least interesting. He was like Hawkins in that he understands and respects musicianship, but I would rather hear, say, Fats Waller. At his best Tatum could get to anybody, including me, but his music lacked momentum. Fats Waller had a tone second to none, whereas Peterson had Bird's idea of swing but had a technique that was European. Then there's Tristano, whose ideas interested me because he was able to construct a solo on the piano, and I guess that has a lot to do with why I had dug Brubeck too. Brubeck was the other half of Tristano; Tristano had the line thing and Brubeck had the harmonic density that I was looking for, and that gave a balance.

But when I heard Horace, now that was a thing which turned me around and finally fixed my idea of piano playing. Horace was playing with Getz. Getz was all over the sax, and Horace was right on him. Listening to Horace that night I dug that there were two attitudes in jazz, one white and one black. The white idea is valid in that the cats playing it play the way their environment leads them, which is the only way they can play. But Horace is the Negro idea because he was playing the real thing of Bud, with all the physicality of it, with the filth of it, and the movement in the attack. Yet Horace supposedly had no technique, which again brings us to the idea of what technique is.

Walter Bishop was also an influence on me. Bird was in town, and Walter Bishop was working with him. Sometimes Bird would show, sometimes not. When he didn't, Walter Bishop would have to carry on the whole thing, and he would do it, man, he really had it. But I think that 1951 was Bishop's undoing, because Horace came to town in '51 and Bishop had been until then reputed to be Bud's descendant. But you couldn't deny Horace. Bishop had Bud's line, but Horace's phrases were short and angular, and finally had more music.

I'm digging the whole scene then. My consciousness was beginning to get to the decisive point. Then I went to Birdland one night to hear Brubeck playing opposite Horace Silver, and I noticed Brubeck imitating Horace. Then came Bird with Percy and Milt, and man, like they demolished Brubeck. Bird was acting grand that night. We would take a solo, step back, and Milt would tear the vibes up. Milt was one of the real forces on that early scene. Well, that ended Brubeck for me. And it ended my emotional involvement with his music and my intellectual involvement also.

I started to dig also that you can't separate the music from the people. Like, when I heard Bird there were people around the bandstand, and even though the music was strong it didn't stop the most creative dancers from moving with it, from trying to create new patterns to fit that new sound that they heard. The reason that the dancing stopped is because the businessman has made the separation complete in terms of who can be the most responsive to the music.

In '52 or '53 I got a group together with an alto saxophonist named Kenny Hyers and with Earl Griffith playing vibes and a drummer named Jack Wilson who used to live over on 118th Street. Well, that was not much of a band, except that Kenny played alto and had a sound like Lee Konitz and Charlie Parker combined, and Earl played, you know, he was interested in investigating things. I was playing my pieces with an eye to changing things, using what I learned from Tristano and others, getting outside the thirty-two-measure structure. Or trying to come to grips with bebop and at the same time trying to get to a different kind of rhythmic pattern.

The band didn't work much, didn't work at all, I don't think. Well, sections of it may have worked occasionally. We did have a lot of rehearsals, and we really grooved ourselves. We had an audition with Foots Thomas for a country gig which didn't happen. Foots Thomas used to play saxophone, had an office in, I think, the Strand Building; a jive cat, you know, like, an occasional kind of scene with promises and then nothing. He told us that we would have to change our thing if we were going to get booked out of his office. I remember Kenny wrote a beautiful tune out of "Sweet Georgia Brown"; it started with the changes and then went its own way. When we played that we were knocked out by it. Foots said, "What is this that you cats are playing!" That's the way it was, more or less.

Earl and I worked together a few times. We'd always end up fighting. The pressure of our differences finally got to the bandstand, and we always ended up cussing each other out. We had a gig way the hell out in New Jersey at Tony Galento's place; John Orr was the third member of that trio, and three more unlikely cats, man, you've never seen. John at that time was reticent, but petulantly so. He just didn't want you to talk with him. I, of course, was very pragmatic about everything, insisting that everything be just so, and Earl always had a sense of humor but always had his own arrogance too, because he didn't want to be tied down by anybody.

So, like, we played the first set and then we'd go, "Well, alright," and then something would happen in the second set, and I'd say, "What are you doing?" and Earl would go into his thing and we'd have a discussion on the bandstand. Poor John. He had begun to play with Bud Powell by this time, and he wasn't accustomed to this. You know, he had the attitude that when you got on the bandstand, you played; you didn't have verbal discussions about aesthetic points of view. And there we were. I still remember that I got salty and walked off the stand, and Earl was scratching his head, and then he walked off another way, and poor John was left to play. A lot like the scene that happened at Birdland the last time Bird was there, actually, only this wasn't Birdland but Fat Tony Galento's in New Jersey. What made it even worse was that to get out to that place you had to travel on a train and then take a local bus. So we were always evil when we got there, and of course we didn't make that much money.

We had one gig at the Art Students League, which was nice. It paid well, and there was always the chance, you know, you always kind of thought that somebody would hear you and make you or some shit like that, but it never happened.

Finally, Earl Griffith decided to go his way, and so did Orr. I told Earl that there were certain things that I was going to do, there were certain harmonic and structural changes that I was going to make, and if anybody wanted to come along, fine, and for those people who didn't, that was also all right, but I was going to find people.

I met Steve Lacy around the time I met Earl. Actually, he was my student, and one of my few consistent sources of income. He had an audition at Birdland and I was supposed to go up with him, but I decided for racial reasons that I didn't want to have an audition with Lacy at Birdland at that time. It would have meant that he was the leader because he had arranged the audition. And in no sense of the word was he ever the leader. So I decided at the last minute not to go, and he was of course very upset about it, justifiably, I suppose. So the audition was cancelled.

We decided to work together when the Transition deal was obvious. In the first place, he went out and got himself a loft. He bought a piano and, in other words, created a rehearsal studio. We worked six or seven weeks there getting the material together so there was no question about what was going to happen on the record. Like, the material was all bound and all we had to do was play, we thought.

I've never been really comfortable in a recording studio. For the most part it's such an artificial situation, and the engineer, of course, makes it even more artificial by the insistence on arranging everybody to fit his idea of sound, which has nothing to do with music, really. A job of pushing buttons, regulating sound, when actually the musician should be the one to tell them what the nature of their sound is, and how the music should sound. In other words, what the engineer should do is simply reproduce the sound after the musicians have set themselves up in the most happy arrangement possible. Then the engineer should try to duplicate the sound that comes out of the arrangements set up by the musicians.*

* Buell Neidlinger remembers: "We went up to Boston to record for that Transition record. We made the Transition recording in a room that wasn't designed for jazz. It was very discouraging because they made our sound by feeding back to the room. The room was designed to record string quartets and other small ensembles: the soft sound, and no drums or saxophones. They produced a sound by taking it off the microphone, feeding it back into the room on loudspeakers, and then taping that. And then they got some resonance, because the room was so dead that for taping jazz it was worthless. It

We went into the Five Spot in 1957, and at that time the scene was simply a very unpretentious place with sawdust on the floor. We followed Dale Wills in there. Dale Wills was a cornet player, and I think he was doing it as an avocation. Dave Amram took me down to play at this place and he said to Joe [Termini], "I think you should hire this man." Joe had a piano that at tops was worth $20. It had no front on it, and the ivory was off some of the keys, but naturally when I played one of the keys broke and one of the hammers flew out and Joe got very upset. That piano was one of the weakest, worst pianos ever conceived by man. Why that piano didn't fall down I'll never know.

Well, anyway, Joe hired us. Actually Joe hired Dick Whitmore, who's a cat from Boston who plays the violin and studied a whole lot of other instruments like that. He got this gig at the Five Spot, and he wanted to use us as his rhythm section. I had started using my Bud Powell style. But after the first night there we got into our thing, and by the third night—it wasn't even the end of the third night—there we were with all this cat's instruments piled on top of the piano,

---

was so confused that they had to put Steve Lacy out into the hallway, practically into another room, because the sound of his soprano saxophone when fed back into the room caused a feedback, a real feedback. So with him out in another room it was a difficult situation. Tom Wilson produced that date, and I think it was one of his first. He thought that he was being very high-leveled by using a very expensive studio which was used for chamber music, etcetera. But actually it would have been better to go down to one of those commercial studios in Boston where they make commercial recordings and they know how to get the sound of an instrument. We spent eight hours in that studio, and in those days that was worth about $150 apiece. He gave us each a check for $41. We were kind of upset. We all came all the way to Boston to do that date, and we didn't get paid expenses or anything. But he didn't have any money really, so I guess that was all he could do.

his violins and his euphoniums and everything, and he was nowhere to be seen. He never came back. It was his gig, and he never came back. Then Lacy came over and started playing with us, and we played there for about seven weeks. I think it would have been much longer except for that damn upright piano of Joe Termini's which he thought was really something. But with the hammers falling out every night and strings breaking he got kind of upset.

Painters like de Kooning, Kline, Larry Rivers, Marisol, and Al Leslie used to leave the Cedar Bar and come over to the Five Spot. When we went in there, the beers were fifteen cents. Within two weeks Joe was throwing out all the derelicts, and prices went up. There was no more sawdust on the floor and there were covers on the tables. When we left he had his club. There was standing room only, and all kinds of people were coming there to hear us. We really made the Five Spot. The group that followed us after that had Valdo Williams in it and was drawing a pretty good salary. [Composer] David Amram wanted me to play with him, but by then I was a leader and I felt that I could never play for him. From Valdo Williams, Termini went to Randy Weston, I think, and then to Charlie Mingus. Later, it was about the summertime, he got Monk, and of course by then he really had it made. At first we made maybe $50 a week for the whole group. When we left he was paying us the minimum union scale. I had some gigs earlier at places like Connie's, the Club Harlem, the Paradise, and places in Newark, but these jobs fell off after the record.

Tom Wilson wound up arranging the next record date I did, that one for United Artists. It was his job to get me to record for United Artists, to engineer the whole thing. I didn't really want to record for Tom Wilson, because by the time I had gotten back to New York from Boston after the

Transition recording I had to bring him up on charges before the union for not fulfilling his contractual obligations. Of course the union decided against me.

But anyway, when the United Artists record date came up I was in such a state of financial despair that I agreed to record for them. Kay Norton, who used to run the Jazz Gallery, at that time was a vice-president of United Artists in charge of the jazz division, and Tom was the *Wunderkind*.

He mentioned using Coltrane on the date, and I said, "Coltrane okay, but I want to use all the musicians that *I* want." I wanted to use Ted Curson, who's a much more contemporary trumpet player than the trumpet player I ended up with, Kenny Dorham. Wilson said that the company had this contract with Kenny Dorham and that they wanted to use him, that a big name might sell more records. So as a leader I had to accept some musicians that I didn't want. That made for what I don't think was a very successful date.

I had anticipated some trouble from Kenny Dorham. He started glaring the minute I walked into the room. He made some subtle and not so subtle statements about the "way-out music" as opposed to the "real thing." So we taped the first tune. We played right through it so there was some life on it, you know, it happened. But by the second tune, "Caravan," Kenny started attacking my playing, and this of course killed any excitement that may have been possible in the date, and the first date is the most important on a recording.

Coltrane I have a lot of respect for. He was involved in trying to find out just what there was in the piano music that he could relate to. He was open to the music since he had just finished playing with Monk at the Five Spot. The thing I dug about 'Trane was that with him it was a matter of music, it was never a matter of personality. Music was all he was concerned with. And as interested as he was in music, he was naturally interested in the machines that recorded it, so that at one point he told Kenny Dorham, "Man, I think you'd get a better sound on the tape if you stood a little closer to the microphone." Well, this just incensed Kenny Dorham, who felt that as the oldest musican present he shouldn't have to be told how to record. He didn't understand the meaning of that remark until at least two hours later, and by that time the entire session had completely degenerated. On that record, only the first tune is an indication of what might have happened.

We even fought over the tunes that we were supposed to play. Myself, I've never been a tune player. That is, I've never found it necessary to memorize two or three hundred tunes. I've always found that if you learn twenty or thirty essential tunes then you have the key.

That was the third record I made. The other was one-half of a record on Verve, taken from the Newport Festival session of the year before. That band that I took to Newport —Steve Lacy, Buell Neidlinger, and [drummer] Dennis Charles—was the first band that employed what I call constructivist principles in music, or what later became constructivist principles. Take the second tune on the Newport recording, "Nona's Blues." I've had musicologists ask me for a score to see the pedal point in the beginning of that piece. They wanted to see it down on paper to figure out its structure, its whole, but at that point I had stopped writing my scores out. I had found that you get more from the musicians if you teach them the tunes by ear, if they have to listen for changes instead of reading them off the page, which again has something to do with the whole jazz tradition, with how the cats in New Orleans at the turn of the century made their tunes. That's our thing, and not composition. There are periods when I go through that and periods when I don't, depending on the score and the musicians. But "Nona's Blues" I did not write out. And the musicologists found that hard to believe, since on that tune one section just flows right into the next. That gives the lie to the idea that the only structured music possible is that music which is written. Which is a denial of the whole of human expression.

We had been working toward this idea of construction for over a year and a half. It began by playing tunes. We used a lot of Monk's tunes in those early days. We used to take the Monk tunes out of themselves into the area in which I was going. This could not really be defined musically, I am unable to define it musically. But by that time I had already developed a method. By 1957 I had a systematic approach. I had been working on this approach for about six or seven years, but I wasn't able to see how I could consciously relate these things. "Tune Two," which we played up in Newport, is like the improvised section to a very involved piece. "Tune Two" is all about changes; it is the logical evolution of the ultimate changes. "Tune Two" and another piece called "Catalyst" were all written pieces.

They were the beginning of the conscious written-down feeling of all that I had done. Even then, composition is subjugated to the feeling of jazz—they swung, "swing" meaning the traditional coloring of the energy that moves the music. It is the physicality of the musician, and the physicality of the musician is determined by the particular tradition that he comes out of—by the blues. Which again brings us back to Ellington, from whom I derived most of my approach to structure and music, even down to the mannerisms, which are personal with me as they are personal with Ellington. These mannerisms of Ellington can be heard in his music just as my own can be heard in my music. There are certain values here. If you listen to Ellington's records, particularly his blues, you can determine these values, and they can be found in the life that he lived. This is particularly true of the music that he wrote in the Forties, and relates to the whole organization of that band.

Again, it's Ellington who influenced my concept of the piano as an orchestra, which meant that the horn players and all of the other players other than the piano were in a sense soloists against the background of the piano. It's like studied improvising.

Another reason that that group disbanded after the Newport thing, and this has been true of every group I've had with the exception of the last one, was that the members of the group always felt that whatever the powers that be, the establishment, offered you, you should take and not quibble. Certainly in '56 or before we were very hot, because I was receiving a lot of offers from a lot of different people. It was simply a question of whether I wanted to go along with the program. Norman Granz sent me a contract. One of the clauses in the contract specified that any music recorded was not to be re-recorded by myself for any other company for five years. This is the usual arrangement, but I thought that it was outrageous that somebody would tell me what I could do with my music for any length of time, not to mention five years. So I never signed a contract.

When I recorded with the next company, I had a lot of contractual hassles, but I think I was proved right because, like, now I get royalty statements of one dollar or two dollars every four or five years. I mean, even before I could define exactly what it was, I knew those guys were robbing us, and I didn't feel that I should be robbed.

Actually, most of my gigs have been pretty miserable,

and I'm including those jobs like carrying out orders at the delicatessens uptown, the jobs at the record stores, the jobs as dishwasher and short-order cook. I've had a lot of musical gigs that fall pretty much in the same categories. That is, gigs where I didn't get paid at all, where there were fights and the musicians could just barely get out with their instruments, or where the instruments were stolen on the job. The club owners were not, like, very lenient; you had to play forty-five minutes on, then you had fifteen minutes off in those gigs—you know, clockwork.

Some of the gigs I've had working uptown, Harlem uptown, were gigs for five dollars, and you worked from eight until four in the morning. This was in the early 1950's. Usually my gigs earned between eight dollars and thirty dollars, and if you got a gig for thirty dollars that was usually a West Indian dance and all the cats you played with played West Indian music.

But that was a gas in its own way. Most of the gigs averaged between ten and fifteen dollars, and you really played. I played with cats who used to walk the bar and honk and carry on and there was no way left for you to play because you had to lay down that shit for them so that they could do their thing. If you didn't lay it down you'd get a calling down or you'd be fired on the spot. And that was all right too. Because, like I say, you had to play, you had to make that thing for them. Even then you didn't have the chance to play for too many dances. The dancing was, like, special events by social clubs, and then you'd get a chance to see the bourgeois Sugar Hill society. They usually appeared at the West Indian things where the music was less to the point, you know. These Sugar Hill people would usually start out the dance very bourgeois, very cool; but then they'd get a little drunk and you'd put the music on them and they'd get out on the floor and they'd do all kinds of impossible things. As for singers, well, some were good but most were indifferent and the remaining were bad. But it was happening, it was happening.

I had one gig at one of those black resorts with Rudy Collins and Steve Lacy and a trumpet player whose name I don't remember, in 1953 or '54, sometime around there. A lot of people like Noble Sisle were up there, and a couple of well-known Negro models. It was a beautiful place.

One thing that I learned from Ellington is that you can make the group you play with sing if you realize each of the instruments has a distinctive personality; and you can bring out the singing aspect of that personality if you use the right timbre for the instrument. It was also the realization of some things that I had learned from Monk—that is, the placing of the chords in relation to the bass and the drum, especially the bass, and steady element. Monk plays very subtly, more subtly than the eighth-note playing of the boogie-woogie pianists and of some contemporary players. As a result, he can jar you emotionally. A horn player playing with Monk must think faster, must think instantly, and Monk does not overblow. That was something that I was working on about that time.

After my father died, I went into analysis. It was Sullivan analysis, a kind of analysis that built on the theory of interpersonal relationships. The analyst would help steer your course. There is a relationship between the analysis and my music, even though it's hard to define. The fact is that, being a musician, I had put a lot of things into music that the music itself was not able to resolve. That is, music is the creation of a language out of symbols, of sounds, sounds that cannot be spoken and therefore create a kind of personal isolation. If there are problems that music cannot answer wholly, you either have to have friends whom you can trust not to destroy you with whatever you give them of yourself, or you have to go to a neutral source, and that is what analysis was for me.

Out of it I gained less concern with guilt. I lost perhaps ninety percent of my guilt, and I could go ahead and do what I felt I had to do. Having come to grips with what I felt guilty about, I was freer to develop my music, though I can't say how much of a difference it made. There was a definite change in the music, a change that was not, unfortunately, recorded. Of course I can't be too sure whether this change would have happened anyway, but because these things happened concomitantly, who can say? But at any rate, around that time the structure of my music became clearer. I went once a week in 1956 for about a year until just before the Newport concert. I started again in February 1959 and went once or twice a week until we went to Europe in 1962. I finally stopped in 1963.

In the Sixties, gigs for me have been mostly, like, a concert a year, filled in with one or two short nightclub or coffeehouse gigs. The coffeehouse gigs may or may not have paid, and if they did pay at all they paid very little.

The concerts have for the most part been produced by people who had no professional experience and therefore knew very little about what they were doing. The '63 Lincoln Center concert was the last time I have played with Sonny Murray, who had by then developed into an immensely important drummer because he could do certain things with time that were not regulated by meter. The idea of the drum as a metronome is finished, and Sonny was one of the first drummers to realize that and to develop a new approach. It was also the last time that Albert Ayler played with me.

The next concert at Town Hall was a musical success but a financial flop. The guy who put it on had no idea how to go about it. He had never done it before, and even though he was well-meaning enough, it would have been better to have gotten someone else to do it—that is, even though his intention was to promote my music and even though he wanted to give most of the profits to me, I still had to stay on his back about getting anything done, and we even had some hassles over the tapes of the concert. But I think that group, like, got to it. I could feel the tradition in our music that night. We had it all. Andrew Cyrille, who is learned enough on his instrument to play with a symphony orchestra, played extremely well, and there were points in which we would get into, like, a pure idealistic thing. The same was true for the rest of the group, particularly Jimmy Lyons, who is a thorough musician and a very fine alto player. That's about it. This summer I did make some more of the festivals: the *Down Beat* festival, the Monterey festival, and the Newport festival, and of course those festivals often turn into circuses in that the music usually turns out to be secondary. But it's, like, an opening, and it pays.

II. ORNETTE COLEMAN

IN THE JAZZ circles of New York in the fall of 1959, there was an unusual feeling of apprehension and anticipation in the air. There was a musician coming, Ornette Coleman, whose singular ear had developed a style of playing that had already been described by highly authoritative sources as the first truly original concept of saxophone playing since Charlie Parker (with the possible exception of John Coltrane). He was reported to be gifted with a musical syntax which, though necessarily derived from Charlie Parker, was a copy of no one, and was in fact a kind of syntax that others must eventually copy. He was a walking myth, the image of a small bearded man striding out of the woods of Texas and into New York's usually closed jazz scene, with a band of acolytes who played only toy instruments. Everything about this man was distinctive: his style of playing, his style of dress, his personal history, his instrument, even his name. Ornette Coleman was to be the very embodiment of both the jazz tradition and of bebop, he who would blow away the fog that seemed to mire down his generation, and provide the light for all who followed.

Strict boundaries had formed around the frontiers of jazz improvisation; and seemingly only two men, John Coltrane and Cecil Taylor, had the heart to go beyond them. Ornette Coleman would change all that.

The first of the rave notices that built up the Coleman mystique came from no less a figure than John Lewis, the leader of the Modern Jazz Quartet, which had been one of the two or three most successful groups of the Fifties. Lewis and the MJQ bassist, Percy Heath, had been helpful in introducing Ornette Coleman to Nesuhi Ertegun of Atlantic records, the producers of the MJQ recordings, and in arranging through Atlantic a paid trip East and a scholarship for him at the Lenox (Mass.) School of Jazz. Both Lewis and Heath went around telling everybody who would listen— which includes almost everyone in the jazz industry—that alto saxophonist Ornette Coleman and trumpeter Don Cherry were potentially two major movers in jazz. The summer before Ornette's New York opening, Lewis was interviewed in an Italian jazz magazine about new trends in jazz: "There are two young people I met in California—an alto player named Ornette Coleman and a trumpet player named Don Cherry. I've never heard anything like them before. Ornette is the driving force of the two. They're almost like twins; they play together like I've never heard anybody play together. It's not any ensemble that I've ever heard, and I can't figure out what it's all about yet. Ornette is, in a sense, an extension of Charlie Parker, and the first I've ever heard. This is the real need I think has to take place, to extend the basic ideas of Bird until they are not playing an imitation but actually something new. I think that they may have come up with something, not perfect yet, and it's still in the early stages, but nevertheless very fresh and interesting."

The Lenox School of Jazz was the laboratory at which Coleman and Cherry were tested, and its faculty that year was impressive. It included clarinetist-composer Jimmy Giuffre, serial composer Gunther Schuller, pianist Bill Evans, John Lewis and Percy Heath, the great bebop drummer Max Roach, and many others. According to the second Ornette Coleman rave notice, Martin Williams' "Letter From Lenox" in the *Jazz Review*, practically all that Coleman had to do was to avoid being led astray by the critics; there was no doubting the fact that Ornette was already an innovator.

Williams and some others talked Joe Termini, the owner of New York's Five Spot, into hiring Coleman for a two-week engagement. Coleman wired plane tickets to his bassist, Charlie Haden, and his drummer, Billy Higgins, and Joe Termini arranged an early evening press conference at the Five Spot for the Ornette Coleman Quartet to show off its innovations. Thus, in the fall of 1959, on a chilly autumn evening, the New York jazz establishment faced its most serious challenger since Charlie Parker came out of Kansas City in 1939. George Hoefer of *Down Beat* reported: "Some walked in and out before they could finish a drink, some sat mesmerized by the sound, others talked constantly to their neighbors or ordered with a drink in hand at the bar. It was, for all, the largest collection of VIP's the jazz world has seen in many a year. A sampling included John Hammond, John Mehegan, Marshall Stearns, John Lewis, Burt Kovell, Eric Vogel, Hsio Wen Shih, Gunther Schuller, Symphony Sid, Pete Long, Bob Riesner, and the Ertegun brothers."

Comments like the following were heard: "He'll change the entire course of jazz." "He's a fake." "He's a genius." "I can't say, I'll have to hear him a lot more times." "He has no form." "He swings like hell." "I'm going home to listen to my Benny Goodman trios and quartets." "He's out, real far out." "I like him, but I don't have any idea of what he's doing."

Hoefer himself did not particularly like what he heard, though he admitted that it was new, different, and honest. He concluded: "Jazz can well use a new thrill, idea, or sound, something similar to what happened when a jaded swing era spawned Charlie Parker, Thelonious Monk, and Dizzy Gillespie. But many critics feel that he is back where Parker was in the groping period."

Few people have been able to get next to Ornette Coleman's music in one hearing. There is just too much personality in his playing to relate its most salient sound to what even the most studiously prepared listener is accustomed to hearing, from any direction. Yet, everyone who attended the first press conference at the Five Spot came prepared to form a lasting opinion. Since then, some of those opinions have changed and some have not. But few of his original detractors consider Ornette a fake today, and this holds true even for those who still do not like his music.

At any rate, the original predictions that Ornette Coleman would change the direction of jazz proved to be completely true. Such modernists as John Coltrane and Jackie McLean admit that hearing Ornette has opened their own ears to new rhythmic possibilities in both group and solo playing. More important is the impact that Ornette's group has had on the generation of musicians who followed them. These younger musicians are overhauling jazz in much the same way the beboppers did, and they are just as controversial. There have been innumerable articles written pro and con on this new music, which was somewhat negatively

named the "New Thing," as if it were a science-fiction mon-
ster.

This impact, however, was not merely technical or, as
LeRoi Jones wrote, "theoretical." There are only one or two
of the horn players generally associated with the new music
whose sounds at all approximate that of Ornette Coleman, or
who play Ornette Coleman licks. This probably can be at-
tributed to the fact that Ornette is almost entirely self-
taught, and that many of his followers have a greater technical knowledge of the saxophone than he does.

Martin Williams' words from the Lenox School of
Jazz concerning Ornette's use of "love" and Ornette's con-
fession that he doesn't "know how it's going to sound before
I play it" have fingered Ornette's true innovation. The discovery had gone out of bebop—it had become as formalistic
as any movement does once it has solved its original problem.
It was that indefiniteness of not knowing how the music is
going to sound before it is played that enhanced its emotional expression. Thus the new musician has been primarily
involved in the cultivation of the Marvelous. And he judges
his work more by the frequency with which the Marvelous
occurs than by compositional values. It is therefore fair
to say that Ornette Coleman's contribution to modern American music has been that he has opened up the way for the
creation of situations wherein incredibly beautiful accidents
occur. However, Ornette's 1966 Blue Note recordings from
Stockholm as well as his June, 1966 trio concert at Lincoln
Center show that this "pure" music has developed into a
virtuosity in which the climaxes are set up as carefully as in
a symphony.

Ornette Coleman was born in Fort Worth, Texas,
March 19, 1930. His mother is a seamstress, and his father

was, as far as Ornette knows, a baseball player. "I don't know who he played baseball for, but the only picture I've ever seen of him was in a baseball uniform." He died when Ornette was seven. Ornette's mother told him that his father could sing, and that he used to sing around Fort Worth, but Ornette doesn't remember this.

He lived for some years with his mother and sister; another sister and a brother had died. His drummer, Charlie Moffett, recalls that Ornette's people were "very sweet, you could always go around to his house and play." Prince Lasha, an avant-garde flutist from Fort Worth, also remembers that while his and Moffett's mothers were constantly complaining about the teen-age musicians "raising so much hell in the living room," it was Ornette's house that was best known among the teen-age jammers as a place to practice without interference from the family.

Ornette recalls hearing music everywhere: "I used to go around in the neighborhood and hear guys playing kazoos and various kinds of odd instruments, combs for example, making up all kinds of music, but I didn't really get into any kind of music myself until my first year at high school." He had to live with seeing all of his friends joining a church band and taking up instruments. Although he begged his mother for a horn, she was too broke to afford it. Ornette persisted, and his mother, indulgent of her only surviving son, finally told him that if he got a job and started bringing some money home, she would see what she could do about a saxophone. He did, and she did. "One night she woke me up and told me to look under the bed, and there was an alto saxophone. I had never touched a horn before." He was about fourteen. But even earlier, Ornette had been fingering a horn.

His cousin, who had been giving saxophone lessons,

often would leave his instrument around the house, and Ornette would pick it up and experiment with it until he was able to play by ear saxophone solos from whatever records there were on hand at the moment. "I must have had a pretty good ear, because about a year later I was making jobs. If some rhythm-and-blues tune would come out I would learn it on the horn and go right out and play it in a nightclub in a dance band."

At about three o'clock one morning, a tenor player, Weldon "Schoolboy" Hagerty, came to Ornette's house, woke the family, and asked if he could borrow Ornette's horn. "Schoolboy" was working in one of the many gut-bucket honky-tonks one finds in a Southern city the size of Fort Worth. He needed a horn to make his gig, and Ornette, who had always heard that Hagerty was one of the leading local musicians, was anxious to hear him play. Ornette's mother was, of course, reluctant to let her son's horn go, but he told her that Hagerty would pay him a ten-dollar rental fee for it, which was untrue. When his mother worried that the horn, which was worth a lot more than ten dollars, might get lost, Ornette convinced her that he should go along with the horn and pick it up when Hagerty had finished playing. She was highly doubtful about letting her teen-age son go to such a place of ill repute, but again the will of the house's only surviving male prevailed. Soon after, Ornette Coleman, still in high school, was making gigs of his own.

Ornette played alto for a year, until he broke his collarbone in a sand-lot football game (Charlie Moffett remembers him as fast and shifty). The accident made practicing impossible and caused him to miss a year of high school. On his return, he joined the school band as a tenor saxophonist. Like many jazz musicians who got their original musical training in their high school bands, Ornette received some further instruction on the saxophone and refined his reading techniques there. It has been suggested that he learned the alto saxophone from a piano book and decided that the A in the book was the C on his horn, that it was this that caused him to have the unusual sense of pitch that is so apparent in his playing. It was in the church and school bands that such self-taught misconceptions were corrected.

There were in the school band some musicians who, like Ornette, were playing rhythm-and-blues and jazz on their instruments outside of school. King Curtis was one; Curtis and Coleman played both jazz and rhythm-and-blues tenor saxophone then, but neither made a distinction between the two styles at the time. Curtis was later to make a large reputation as an R-&-B tenor saxophonist and then to switch back to jazz, becoming, as someone once remarked, an "AC-DC musician." Charlie Moffett, who was later to tour Europe as Ornette Coleman's drummer, was playing trumpet in that school band. Prince Lasha played saxophone; he and Ornette were called "jazzhounds" and were finally dismissed from the band for jazzing the "Washington Post March." Ornette was deeply offended, as he had been completely innocent on that particular occasion, though he laughingly admits that he had jazzed other tunes before without the director's catching him at it. Lasha came north after high school and gigged around Chicago and some other midwestern cities. Along with Sonny Simmons, an alto saxophonist, he came to New York in 1962 as a flutist, and they were two of the first "post-Ornette Coleman" reedmen to hit the scene. They were, in fact, the only two musicians to use Ornette's personal instrument, the white plastic alto saxophone (actually, Charlie Parker had played a plastic alto years earlier). Lasha recorded with Simmons, with his own group, and worked with John Coltrane and Sonny Rollins.

All these teen-agers worked the Fort Worth black night-spots, but you would not have recognized them at the time. Ornette now dresses relatively conservatively, notwithstanding a taste for odd hats. But the style of the black South in the mid-Forties was dominated by the Cab Calloway–Billy Eckstine image. The Dizzy Gillespie look was only for magazine consumption; and even though Ornette and his friends did hear Gillespie, they never wore the berets and leopard-skin jackets that adorned him on the *Ebony* covers. Cab Calloway's zoot suit was a reality in the South, as was Billy Eckstine's famous wing-shaped "Mr. B." collar. Zoot was the "unborn calf" and "knob" shoe, the fuzzy beaver hat, the "neat seat with the reet pleat" pants, pegged to seven inches. Ornette Coleman's jacket had thickly padded shoulders and patch pockets with flaps. His hair was "conked" (the curl glued out of it with a gelatinous substance called Konkoline) and combed backward flat down on his head until it formed a thick shiny surface. That was Ornette then, smaller than his suit: long pointed lapels, shoes either needle-pointed unborn calf or long, slim, squared-upturned-toe "knobs" or "rockers."

On the bandstand in those days, Ornette's playing was out of the Lynn Hope or Big Jay McNeely bag—he "went crazy" when he played, doubled over backward with the bell of the horn pointed over his shoulder, jumped up on tables and danced while honking the latest Arnett Cobb solo. Ornette, the teen-age honker and contortionist of the saxophone, acquired a gutbucket essence in his music then which he has never lost.

The arrangements were all copies, mostly by ear, of the rhythm-and-blues groups which were popular at the time. In the honky-tonk and after-hours joints where he worked most often, this was all that was in demand; there was no separation of gutbucket music from any other kind. Among the instrumentalists Ornette used to copy were Big Jay Mc-Neely, Louis Jordan, Arnett Cobb, and Gene Ammons. Prince Lasha was the singer and alto saxophonist of the group, Moffett the trumpet player, and Ornette the tenor saxophonist. The others came from a rotating list of approximately a dozen musicians of all ages. When Lasha sang, he sounded like Louis Jordan on the Louis Jordan arrangements ("South Port West Virginia" and "I'm Gonna Move Way Out to the Outskirts of Town") and Billy Eckstine on the Eckstine copies ("Prisoner of Love," "Sweet Georgia Brown"). Moffett remembers that Ornette later came to imitate Charlie Parker and Alan Eager, but that it was Louis Jordan and Billy Eckstine who were most in demand. Ornette's sister, Travenza, fulfilled many of the functions of an agent, representing the group and helping to work out a repertoire.

All of the musicians from Fort Worth agree that it was a hustlers' town. There was oil money, cattle money, and textile money, and some of it filtered down to even the lowest classes. It attracted musicians, and all of the major bands came through Fort Worth. Ornette even sat in with Stan Kenton's orchestra once. Nightclubs of all descriptions flourished, and the shadiest ones hired teen-age musicians of dubious professional standing.

During his high school years, then, Ornette spent half his day in school and half his night working in some of the most disreputable nightspots in Fort Worth. If his mother disapproved of her son working in places where people were regularly cut and shot to death and where weekend riots were the norm, what could she do? Ornette usually earned more than one hundred dollars a week—an incredible wage during the Forties, and, as Lasha says, more than any of the high school teachers made—and that went a long way toward supporting the family. Ornette says: "I've seen guys get cut up and shot and killed. I had a high school girlfriend who was finishing school a year before me, and I wanted to take her to the prom. I rented a slick tuxedo and I told my mother I was taking this girl to the prom. Then I got a call to come and work at this honky-tonk place, and we needed the money, so I had to work.

"Like most of the places we worked in, it was mainly a gambling joint—the music was a cover for gambling. When the Texas Rangers would come in, people would run out and start dancing so they couldn't legally take you out and bust [arrest] you. That night was very rough even for that place. A couple of guys got cut up and one was shot and killed. So there I was sitting up in this place in my tuxedo, crying my heart out thinking that the music I was playing was causing these people to cut each other up. I always wanted to get out of there, but I was making maybe a hundred dollars. Coming from a very poor family, living by the railroad track, well, you can figure that one out.

"Anyway, I was more or less supporting my mother and sister and doing what I thought was right. I don't know what finally happened to that girl."

Moffett, who had started playing in those nightclubs at the age of thirteen, finished high school at fifteen and went into the Navy, where he became welterweight boxing champion. Lasha finished high school in the same year and went north. Ornette stayed behind in Fort Worth—set back a year in school by that broken collarbone—jamming with every musician he could find. About six of them, he remembers, sounded better than anybody he has heard before or since, and of these, Red Connors was a major influence on the development of his thought and work.

Red Connors is a tenor and alto saxophonist who Ornette insists was doing in the mid-Forties much of what John Coltrane is doing in the Sixties, but in a gutbucket style. After Coleman's own group disbanded, he came to work several times in a large group led by Connors, who must have seen some talent in the young tenor man. It was Connors who taught Ornette the value of learning to read music, even though most of the arrangements the band used were "head" arrangements. Ornette says: "The notes that made up the musical passages were the most important thing to him, what notes and what order they were played in. I found this to be a very important asset to me in learning to play music, because with many things, if you don't have it in your head, you might not be able to repeat it. So if you have the notes in your head and you know how to phrase those notes, you can get the passage that you played before. I never saw Red and those others writing music down, that is, writing compositions, but they did have musical knowledge of what they were doing."

It was Connors who introduced Ornette Coleman to the phenomenon of bebop and thus taught him the difference between popular jazz and serious jazz. Ornette had until then been entirely under the influence of local musicians and of the big-name R-&-B artists. Although he was to continue working primarily as a rhythm-and-blues musician during the remainder of his professional period in Texas, he did get to play bebop arrangements in Connors' band whenever circumstances would allow. Ornette says: "I heard them play every bebop tune that was recorded between 1943 and 1950. They could play any other composition by any other major guys who were writing bebop music. I knew most of the

tunes; I could play those that Bud Powell and Charlie
Parker had written and George Shearing had written. Anything that was melodically complicated I thought I had to
learn—a bunch of bebop tunes."

When Fats Navarro died in 1950, Ornette remembers
hearing about it while on a gig and wondering why he was
still in Fort Worth playing rhythm-and-blues. The first
Charlie Parker tune he ever heard was "Now Is the Time,"
which he thought was "The Hucklebuck." Since "The
Hucklebuck" and "Now Is the Time" were the same tune,
reasoned Coleman, then bebop and rhythm-and-blues must
be the same kind of music: "The only other kind of music
besides hillbilly music I knew is what is known as classical
music. And I never heard much of that in Fort Worth except in the music-appreciation classes in high school where
they would play a classical record every now and then. It
seemed to me like a commercial or something, I mean I
couldn't connect the life that I was living in Fort Worth to
classical music. I always thought of classical music as organized reading, no one instrument ever stood out as the
performer having something to do with the performance."

There were musicians who passed through Fort Worth
in a seemingly unending stream, and Fort Worth seemed
to be the kind of place for many of them to get stranded.
Ornette would play with anybody passing through who
would let him, and this broadened his perspective considerably.

Lester Young was one musician who sometimes stayed
over in Fort Worth. (Ornette thought then that Lester
Young's and Charlie Parker's phrasing in ballads was very
similar.) Ornette and "Schoolboy" Hagerty went down to
hear their hero, Red Connors, sit in with Lester Young on
one of these occasions and, thinking back on it, Ornette feels

that Young must have been in one of those periods when he had no inspiration, for they came away convinced that Connors was the better horn player. It was only much later when he heard Young's records that he realized that there was something in Young's playing that he hadn't shown that night, when he had only been interested in playing a kind of blues "where you ride the same note for about forty to fifty bars."

Ornette recognized a gradual process of change taking place in his approach to music during those years. It was as if the bebop movement filtered down almost invisibly from those urban centers where it was being consciously worked out. Ornette in Texas felt the excitement, the technical changes, and a vague sense of the meaning of the new approach taken to music and to the musical audience by jazz musicians during that era: "During the Forties, I think, the whole music structure of America was turned on by bebop. But I had heard those local musicians before I heard bebop, and when I heard bebop it sounded at first like they were just playing more notes. Then I realized that in bebop they would take a song form and the changes and write another melodic line. I thought that was the greatest thing since Bach, that it was a real advancement, which it was. Then I started getting involved in learning song-form music and then writing different melodic lines on top of the chord changes myself. It was nice to be able to play 'Jumping at the Savoy' changes and put another melodic line across. I thought that that was a very inventive form of playing, and I thought everybody that was interested in playing music that way was doing that: Bud Powell, Charlie Parker, Dizzy Gillespie, and, of course, Thelonious Monk, who was and is the master of taking the chord change of a tune and playing a different melodic line on top of it."

Ornette's experience had been in all-black nightspots where the music was the hardest, raunchiest gutbucket. The music the white joints of Fort Worth wanted from the local jazz musicians was significantly more genteel than the kind Ornette had thought of as inspiring the black people to kill each other, and it may be significant that the first performance in which he realized he was going to be involved in playing a new music occurred at one of the latter establishments.

Ornette's band had broken up, and in 1948 he had taken the alto-saxophone seat in Red Connors' band in an all-white place, his first such job: "One night I was playing 'Stardust' —the alto saxophone always plays the lead in 'Stardust'— and I was dragged because I could hear all these other notes that I could play to the changes of 'Stardust.' The people were out there just slow dragging, so I just nutted out and started playing all the things I could think of to the changes without touching the melody. And then a guy hollered out: 'Get on the melody, get on the melody!' and then I realized: 'Why should I have to stick to the melody when I was already playing the melody and this guy didn't know it?' That's when I started investigating other possibilities of playing music without having any straight guidelines as far as changes or chords are concerned."

Could this concern with new possibilities in music be a partial reaction to a racist audience? Ornette vividly remembers: "I had a beard and my hair was thicker than it is now, and this fellow came up to me and said, 'Say, boy, you can really play saxophone. I imagine where you come from they call you mister, don't they?' He couldn't see me with my hair and beard coming from Texas; Negroes don't go around looking like that. So I said, 'No, this is my home.' 'I want to shake your hand,' he says. 'It's an honor to shake your hand because you're really a saxophone player—but you're still a nigger to me.' That's how sick he was. There's no answer for that, that insanity. Playing in a white place, I couldn't tell him, because I would have been jeopardizing my life."

The progressive development of Coleman's interest in a new music was commensurate with his frequent employment in white establishments. At the same time that drunken club owners were telling him, "I got enough money to burn a wet elephant but I ain't gonna give it away," and offering him three dollars a night to play from nine P.M. until two A.M., Ornette was "trying to analyze everything that I could possibly do to avoid playing changes and chords, and also trying to avoid playing ballads and chords, and also trying to avoid playing ballads simply because it was easy to feel something to play in the next phrase."

And at the same time that he was working in a Texas club where a white woman cornered him in the kitchen during an intermission and raised her dress over her head— which made him know that his life would be over if a white man passed by—he was "trying to find ways to play things that I heard right on the spot, yet make them sound as though I had practiced them and polished them up." The situation in the white clubs was simple: "I thought that as long as they were white, they all had the same thing in common, to control and rule you."

The music he was trying to play for his own satisfaction had a place in none of the white clubs and in few of the Negro clubs. Furthermore, Texas was getting harder to take, though it would still be a couple of years before he'd be able to leave it. Ornette told Joe Goldberg: "People in Texas, they are so wealthy, it's still like slavery. You had to be a servant. You had to be serving somebody to make some money. When

I finished high school all the kids I knew who had been to college and come back, they had porter's jobs. What's the reason of going to college? That's the reason I didn't go. You've got to try to get a job teaching in the colored school system, or that's it. People have been teaching there for fifty years, you have to wait for them to die. I didn't come from a poor family, I came from a po' family, poorer than poor. Even the principal where I went to school worked in the summer in the hotel where I worked as a busboy. I saw him doing some things, I didn't have respect for him."

Ornette "realized around then that I would have to leave Fort Worth and Texas altogether. But I had never spent any time away from home and I couldn't really think of what it would be like to leave Texas, or how to go about it."

So he spent the next year gigging in Fort Worth, listening to "guys like Roy Brown, Charles Brown, Lonnie Johnson, and Gatemouth Moore. Joe Turner came to Fort Worth and stayed about two or three months, and I backed him with my band for a couple of months there. That's the only kind of music I would play in public, for singers who were singing the blues."

Actually, Ornette's first gig outside Fort Worth had come a few years earlier in Amarillo, Texas. A Negro club owner from Amarillo, named Carter, came to Fort Worth and heard Ornette in one of those after-hours clubs where he was gaining a reputation as a hard-blowing saxophonist. He decided that Ornette was the perfect complement for his house band in Amarillo and that he would have him at any cost. That particular band was led first by a guitarist named Rudy Green, who left for New York after a few engagements, and then by Moffett, who had become a proficient reader and writer of music in a Navy music school. Ornette had sent for his cousin, James Jordan, a baritone player, and Red

Connors came in from Wichita Falls to play tenor. (There was also a valve trombonist whose name no one remembers.) Moffett remembers that Ornette began to develop about this time as a writer, and composed a tune named the "Berry Cup Shuffle," after Berry Cup wine (15 percent), which Moffett still enjoys playing. In the beginning, Carter had to buy Moffett a set of drums to get the band together, because Ornette insisted that he would not go without him. When the summer ended, Jordan returned to college, and Moffett, who was still eligible for the draft and feeling the hot breath of Korea, decided to enroll in Houston Tillotson College, where he asked for and received a scholarship. Although it was too small to sustain him throughout his four years there, the set of drums Carter had bought for him enabled Moffett to work his way through school.

By 1949, nineteen-year-old Ornette Coleman had come to some kind of an impasse in Fort Worth which he did not understand. Bebop and rhythm-and-blues seemed intransigent musics to him now, although he recognized them as head and feet of the same body. The problem was that he had no outlet for playing and developing his music; but, of course, it was not as simple as all that to him at the time. "I hadn't seen much else; all I knew was that all kinds of things weren't right with me at Fort Worth." His departure from Fort Worth was based more on this growing sense of discontent than on a clear decision to make a break.

The most common means for young musicians anxious to leave their home towns and get into the mainstream of jazz has always been to hook up with a touring band, and that was what Ornette did. His choice was a mistake, and a long-drawn-out trauma for the teen-ager who was still tied tightly to his mother's apron strings.

Ornette had played with several of the bands that had

stopped over in Fort Worth, and he was an energetic, sincere, and obviously talented young musician. But, as Charlie Moffett said, "Ornette was sounding like Ornette by the time he was seventeen," for he had an eccentric, strangely tuned style of playing, whether in rhythm-and-blues or bebop. It is hardly surprising that none of the traveling band leaders of the time proposed to take him on the road with them.

Had he been a more glib musician, Ornette might have found a seat in somebody's reed section, and such a seat might have exposed him to the kind of first-rate musicianship that would have saved him years of isolation. As it was, the only opening he found exposed him to the meanest employment conditions that existed in the entertainment business. Ornette went to work for "Silas Green from New Orleans."

The history of minstrelsy as a force in American culture has been well documented, and here it is necessary to reflect on only a few aspects of it. It is common knowledge that the blackface minstrel—a jealous white parody on Afro-American life—was developed in the last years of antebellum America. This led to the development of the black professional entertainer, who improved on the form; the famous "Juba" (William Henry Lane) was generally acknowledged to be the most famous dancer on the American and European popular stage in the mid-nineteenth century. During Reconstruction, when the freedman became something of a market, the traveling shows, medicine and minstrel, were the only forms of professional entertainment available to them.

Musically, minstrel shows had disseminated a good deal of Afro-American music from city to backwoods, from state to state; whatever homogeneity developed in certain of its forms, notably blues, was largely attributable to minstrelsy.

The blues was spread by such singers as Gertrude "Ma" Rainey, who appeared in Rainey's Rabbit Foot Minstrels. (It was "Ma" Rainey who discovered Bessie Smith and started her on her career.) Instrumental jazz as it was being played in New Orleans was heard in many backwoods areas for the first time when minstrel shows, based in and passing through New Orleans, picked up musicians. Jelly Roll Morton, who worked with the McCabe and Young minstrels in 1910, was one such musician, as was Bunk Johnson, who played with Holcamp's Georgia Smart Set from 1903 to 1931.

By the turn of the century, two kinds of minstrel shows played the South: one was the highly paid variety represented by Mahara's Minstrels (featuring W. C. Handy, by no means a blues musician), which played its own version of "high-class" music and would have nothing to do with the blues; the other played barrelhouse music. As the Silas Green Company advertised in the *Freeman* in March, 1914, "they plays the blues, that's all!"

It was groups such as Silas Green and the Johnson and Johnson's Minstrels that outlived by far the sophisticated black minstrels and the blackface white groups; both had largely disappeared by 1920. As an adolescent in Elizabeth, North Carolina, I recall crawling under the canvas tents of "Silas Green from New Orleans" to watch the semi-naked women do their dances and to hear the comedians' crude but, I thought then, hilariously funny jokes. This was about the same time that Ornette Coleman joined one of the Silas Green troupes, but he never came as far as North Carolina. By 1950 the company was seedy, its canvas tent was ragged, its dancers somewhat shopworn. Elizabeth City was a small enough town (approximately 13,000 population), but the Negroes who lived in it seldom attended Silas Green shows; the group drew its biggest revenue from the "country people" who lined the city streets on weekends. We had radio, and most of the country people did not; we also had a movie house. Fights were frequent, gambling always took place behind the tents, and if a Silas Green group hit town during the summer potato season when the migrant workers were in Elizabeth City, the entire area would be off limits to us "city" kids.

It is not difficult to understand, then, why Ornette had to con his mother into letting him take the job with Silas Green. What he told her was that he had a job "with a guy who wanted to organize a band to go to Dallas." If she had known the real itinerary, she would never had permitted him to go; in the old days, it was known as the T.O.B.A. circuit, named after the *Theatre Owners and Bookers Association;* but the blues people thought it stood for Tough On Black Artists!

Ornette said: "We went to Oklahoma, Georgia, New Orleans, Mississippi, and Little Rock. We played in all-Negro theaters, and in outdoor tents. The music was strictly minstrel music, since we used to play for shake dancers and all that kind of stuff. Most of the guys were from the sort of places we were going to: from Alabama and Mississippi. I was the only guy from Texas. I went to some places, man, and saw some scenes that I hate to even talk about. I thought I had played in some rough places in Fort Worth, those gambling joints and all that, but the scenes we had in that minstrel group were something else. It was the worst job I ever had. I was miserable.

"The comedians were like Uncle Tom-type minstrels. I guess they were good, because the audience used to crack up unless they were too drunk to even hear what was going on. Of course the musicians were all Negro, but they were playing tunes like "Nacky Sacky," "Tiger Rag," and "Twelfth

Street Rag," and other tunes that were like white Dixieland tunes. This was their repertoire. They also played some blues, and I had one solo in the blues.

"Anyway, I traveled all around until we got to Natchez, Mississippi, and I had just heard before we got there that there had been a big fire and lots of Negroes had gotten burned up. We played in a run-down place that had a theater in the back, like, a rear theater. By then all the guys in the band had started to dislike me, being that I was the only guy from Texas, and being that I played different from them. They really hated the way I played.

"So while they were playing in Natchez, I went out to the restaurant to get something to eat. While I was eating I started talking to this guy who was either white or light enough to pass for white, and he told me that he had a record company, Imperial Records, I was told. He asked me to record for them right then, on the spot. The guy picked up some musicians and we went to the studio where I recorded some tunes right off the top of my head. I don't know what happened to them. I'd like to try to run them down sometime.

"While I was in Natchez I tried to show the other tenor player some things. Shit, I was tired of doing all my practicing alone. He went to the bandleader and said I was trying to make him into a bebopper, and the bandleader fired me on the spot.

"So that's where I got fired from the carnival band: in Natchez, Mississippi. Then the law decided that I didn't look right, these white cracker cops. They looked at me and asked me what I was doing there, they knew I wasn't from Natchez. I told them that I had just gotten fired from the carnival band and that I was a musician. They said some pretty horrible things to me, called me some names, told me they didn't need musicians in Natchez, and ran me out of town."

Ornette joined Clarence Samuels' rhythm-and-blues group and toured the South with him for a few months until, late in 1949, he got stranded in New Orleans.

In Baton Rouge the week before, the band had been playing in a roughhouse dancehall. During one of the dances, Ornette decided that he would make one of those intermittent interjections of his own idea of modern music into the middle of his blues solo. All that he accomplished was stopping the dance and touching the nerves of some of the toughest men in the hall.

After the set, a girl walked up to Ornette and told him that someone outside wanted to meet him. Ornette closed his horn case, picked it up, and went out the door. All that he remembers about them now is that "goddam those cats were big." He was standing in darkness on a hill behind the building, near some trees, when at least three men surrounded him, and he knew immediately that they were going to beat him. His first thought was to shield his saxophone case in both arms, and he tried to hide his face behind the case. They pried his arms apart, smashed the case, smashed the saxophone, and threw it off the hill. Then they threw Ornette down, and kicked him. With the exception of a 1962 record date, this was the last time Ornette played tenor saxophone.

Today, Ornette tries to rationalize away the fact that he was beaten because of the way his music sounded, and one recalls his worry that it was his music that had caused people to get cut up and shot in the gambling houses in Fort Worth. He has since evolved a complicated idea of "social love," and he explains events such as the beating in terms of the lack of this all-pervasive "love." But what Ornette thinks of as love in his music has always sounded like something else to many in his audience. (Viz., Miles Davis' famous remark: "Hell, just listen to what he writes and how he plays. If you're talking psychologically, the man is all screwed up inside.")

Incidents like the one in Baton Rouge seemed to follow Ornette around during the entire time he played the tenor saxophone. He became almost mystical about the instrument. He told me: "The tenor is a rhythm instrument, and the best statements Negroes have made, of what their soul is, have been on tenor saxophone. Now you think about it and you see I'm right. The tenor's got that thing, that honk, you can get to people with. Sometimes you can be playing that tenor, and I'm telling you, the people want to jump across the rail. Especially that D-flat blues. You can really reach their souls with that D-flat blues."

So there he was, a tenor saxophonist from Fort Worth strung out in Baton Rouge without a saxophone. He knew someone "up the road," however, so he decided to travel with the band until they reached New Orleans.

Ornette's friend in New Orleans was clarinetist Melvin Lassiter, and he was lucky to have him after the Baton Rouge incident. He looked up Lassiter, told him his trouble, and Lassiter immediately offered him a room in his mother's house. Melvin's brother had recently stopped playing alto and "that's how I started back playing alto. It was while I was staying at Melvin's that I started playing like I'm trying to play now. The things that me and [Don] Cherry were doing, Melvin and I could do that then, and that was 1949."

Ornette says: "I had been practicing and playing with myself during all the time that I was on the road with those minstrels and rhythm-and-blues groups. I had a lot of ideas that I just couldn't keep down. I kept hearing all kind of possibilities and I wanted to play them."

So Ornette's idiosyncrasies developed into a full concept by virtue of his playing in an isolated and strictly gut-bucket context all during his most formative years.

Although New Orleans was better known for having been the "cradle" of the jazz naissance in the prewar turn-of-the-century days, he had heard from Lassiter how many modern musicians there were in the city; and it was during this six-month stay there that Ornette learned just what kind of hostility his music could create among his peers in modern jazz. Before this, he had thought it was only the audience—who insisted on hearing familiar music—who had been hostile to his sound. In New Orleans, he learned that modern musicians could be as biased as the most illiterate backwoods farmer. Lassiter briefed Ornette on the places where modern jazz was played, and introduced him to all the modern jazz musicians around New Orleans at the time. Ornette recalls only two who were open to what he was doing: clarinetist Alvin Batiste (Batiste is now in New York, where he is regarded as an underground giant of the clarinet) and drummer Ed Blackwell, whom Ornette met again in Los Angeles and who later joined him in New York.

Ornette was working nonmusical or day jobs—doing yard work and such—and sitting in whenever he could at night. His music at that time had a lot of Charlie Parker in it, as the prevailing thought was that there were only two ways to play the alto saxophone: like Bird or like Johnny Hodges. Yet there was already an unusual quality in Ornette's interpretation of Bird. He would approach the "head" of the tune from a harmonic angle that sounded dissonant to the rest of the group, a habit which caused many musicians to think that he played constantly out of tune. This misconception was to follow Ornette until the present day. His solos went off in directions the other musicians thought had little to do with the chords, and, again, this freehanded approach to the chord changes of the tunes was to mean that Ornette would spend his mature professional career to date exclusively with musicians who were committed to the same idea of playing.

It was during these six months in New Orleans that Ornette first had to deal with modern musicians walking off the stand when he approached it. Nevertheless, he thinks back on the period as being more positive than not, since he did get to work out some musical ideas with Lassiter and did receive encouragement from two musicians of obviously unusual talent—Ed Blackwell and Alvin Batiste.

Ornette's old Fort Worth employer, Pee Wee Crayton, came through New Orleans in the winter of 1949 with an open seat in his reed section. When Ornette learned that Crayton eventually would stop in Los Angeles before swinging back to Texas, he finagled a saxophone and accepted the job in Crayton's band.

Except for a brief return to Fort Worth in 1953, Los Angeles became Ornette's home for the next nine years. It was a whole new scene for him, his first "northern" city: "I had never been in an all-white place, no more than playing. And I had never been in an all-white place where I wasn't an employee. I was really turned around when I went to California, where I could walk into places without being employed there. I went there in Pee Wee Crayton's band, which also had Red Connors in it. And when we walked into these places it seemed very strange to me not to see the signs up over the bathrooms, to eat in restaurants with white people."

He was later to learn that racial discrimination involved more than signs over the bathrooms and eating in public places. He had some bad experiences with policemen—Los Angeles police are notorious for stopping and searching black people found in wealthy white neighborhoods who cannot prove that they're servants. Such incidents with the Los Angeles police continued during his nine years there, and he reports having been stopped and searched by the police on the streets of Beverly Hills during his band's tour of the coast in 1964.

Reflecting on the differences in his experiences as a black man in Los Angeles and in the South, Ornette says: "The Negro who is born in California is a different type of Negro, he just automatically assumes that it's not happening. But in Los Angeles, all Negroes that the cops haven't seen before are stopped and searched. That's a bad scene. I was going to look up the chief of police and tell him what I thought about the setup out there. Human behavior cannot be dictated like that. You just can't see somebody walking down the street and decide that you want to search him. Any police commissioner who gives his men that authority —any city that gives its policemen that authority—is a police state. That's not right, and being a Negro, I find that under the law of California, a white cop can stop me just because I look out-of-the-ordinary to him. Lots of white Southern people go out to California, and they get to own things and they get the place all screwed up, confusing what it means to be comfortable with controlling. California is just a bad place for anyone who is trying to develop a form of expression in which prejudice does not play a part."

Crayton must have been horrified at the musical turn his old protégé had taken, as he was paying Ornette *not* to play by the time they reached Los Angeles. Again, Ornette was stranded in a strange city with no money, few friends, and no work. He moved into the Morris Hotel on Los Angeles' Fifth Avenue. "Skid Row," he calls it, though it was not nearly that bad. The Morris is a formerly elegant hotel that the neighborhood changed on, "a run-down Hotel

Theresa," as Ed Blackwell describes it. The hotel attracted all the jazz musicians who weren't making it, and quite a few of those who had come to Los Angeles on the road were in residence. The Morris would seem, then, an excellent place for an obscure young musician to make connections of lasting importance, a clearinghouse where Ornette might cut himself into the musicians stationed around Los Angeles and pick up with leaders who might be going on the contemporary T.O.B.A. circuit. For Ornette, it was nothing of the sort.

As it happened so often later, the men around Ornette in Los Angeles took sides about him as a musician and as a man almost immediately. Ornette is a small and frail man, and at the age of twenty-four he was still suffering from the collarbone injury that had not healed properly after the accident that had occurred more than five years before; this may partially explain why some of the "brothers" in the hotel took advantage of him. As he had been unable to find either a night or day gig in his first few months in Los Angeles, Ornette had had to rely for meals largely on canned goods sent to him from home by his mother. As he would always share what he had with the others, before long the other musicians in the hotel began to know when to expect shipments of food from Fort Worth. Ornette received a cake from home on his twenty-fifth birthday. The musicians crowded around him and took it away from him with a round of good-natured but serious threats. Ornette had to stand aside and watch the cake, which he had more than a sentimental attachment for, being devoured. As Blackwell says, "The cake, like it wasn't that important, but Ornette was hungry and pretty lonesome, and it was from home. And he had had a hard time traveling through the South."

After the cake incident, Ornette wired his mother for

money to come back to Fort Worth. He found the town the same except that many of his old associates had left it, which only made a bad situation worse; after two uneventful years he decided to make his stand again in Los Angeles in 1952.

This time he moved in with a friend in the Watts ghetto, some distance from downtown Los Angeles. His existence during this period was one of desolation, in which he "ate and slept whenever I could." He would regularly make the long walk from Watts to downtown Los Angeles to hear what was happening in the clubs and to sit in occasionally. During his first stay in Los Angeles, when he still had been playing a cross between his own brand of rhythm-and-blues and bebop, he had sat in with Teddy Edwards, Hampton Hawes, Sonny Criss, and other Los Angeles-based musicians at a place called the Dixie Club on Broadway. Ornette says that Edwards and the others liked his playing at that time, although some other musicians who were around Los Angeles in those days testify that Ornette was disliked even then. This second time around, however, when Ornette's music was getting closer to maturing, the jazz musicians of Los Angeles were almost unanimous in putting it down. His supporters among the musicians were very few, and those who did support him became fast friends and, for the most part, accomplices. Drummer Edward Blackwell, who had been an inmate with Ornette at the Morris, was one. Ed Blackwell had been respected in New Orleans as a superior technician, and the Los Angeles musicians had recognized his dexterity too. Blackwell says: "There were certain little things in Ornette's playing in New Orleans that I heard again in Los Angeles and then again in New York. But Ornette sounded a lot like Charlie Parker back then, and he was still hung up with one-two-three-four time. I had been experimenting with different kinds of time and cadences, and since Ornette and I used to share together, we had reached some new grooves. Ornette's sound was changing too, and a lot of the musicians used to think he played out of tune. He never used to play the same thing twice, which made a lot of the guys think that he didn't know how to play."

There were other factors that alienated Ornette from the Los Angeles jazz scene. He was physically conspicuous: He had let his face and head hair grow as long as it could, and he'd straightened and curled his hair. He had started to dress in clothes that were homemade in a fashion no one else wore. Don Cherry says that Ornette "looked like some kind of black Christ figure, but no Christ anybody had ever seen before."

Even Ornette's religion was bizarre for a black jazz musician in Los Angeles; he had joined the Jehovah's Witnesses, "the only organization I've gotten baptized in since I was in the Methodist Church." His conversion was concomitant with his marriage. He had met Jane, a girl who had heard him on one of his infrequent gigs and had subsequently weathered the usual shower of boos to follow him from club to club.

She herself dressed unconventionally, making her own clothes as she later made clothes for Ornette. She was an intelligent girl who was very well read; her record collection was enormous, and unusually informed in that it included the most advanced jazz and classical records of the time. She was also an extremely attractive woman, of mixed Negro and Filipino blood. Her mother had been one of a set of twins and her family was one of the most attractive in the Watts district.

Because of her strong interest in and knowledge of music, Jane's circle of friends included such people as Don Cherry and George Newman, as well as several of the other more adventurous younger jazz musicians around Los Angeles. Cherry says that he knew her three or four years before he knew Ornette, and that he had first heard of Ornette through her. Jane and Ornette had one child, a son, Denardo.

It was, then, not because he was unknown that Ornette was turned away from the nightclub doors on such occasions as the time that he went to try to sit in with Charlie Parker at the Tympani. Ornette was known by then as a "weird" musician in a town that is known for its "weirdies." He says: "I had a beard and long hair and all that stuff. I was kind of taking life as what I thought it was in terms of the values I thought were important. I had a bad reputation for not knowing music. I think basically this was because I was from the South and because the L.A. guys thought they were a lot hipper than anybody from the South could be. I did know a lot of bebop tunes, but I would play them differently and then I would start soloing, so they thought I was all screwed up or something. I didn't do too much socializing. I thought that I was just doing it naturally and trying to follow my own philosophy."

At one point Ornette was approached by some young Communists in L.A. who found jobs for him at three and five dollars a night. Although he soon became disenchanted with them, it was not for ideological reasons: "They made me feel as though they were doing me a great service, simply because I was a guy from Texas and hadn't been exposed to a free life and they were doing me a favor by accepting me in their organization. But I never joined the organization because I couldn't accept the fact that they felt like they had to respect me because that was their responsibility as Communists. I didn't think they were doing me any favor by acting decent because I could tell that if they hadn't been

Communists they would have been prejudiced. It wasn't real. I don't think that any form of social life is real when a person has to find out what you're doing and what your possibilities are before he likes you.

"I don't mean to compare the Jehovah's Witnesses and the Communists as organizations, but I did have a similar experience with the Jehovah's Witnesses. I joined them because I had just gotten married and gotten a kid, and you know their religion is really based on the family. The only thing was that when I went back to Texas for a visit, I called up the Jehovah's Witnesses and a lady told me that they had a colored hall that I could go to. They have an explanation that you're supposed to accept, but I didn't understand it, and I still don't understand it. That hasn't destroyed my belief in God, but I found out that the church needs God just like the people."

After his marriage, Ornette made another strong attempt to find work in the nightclubs. He went down to sit in with tenor saxophonist Dexter Gordon one night and found that Dexter had, characteristically, not shown up in time for the first set. Ornette went up to play with Dexter's rhythm section only to have Gordon come in and order him off the bandstand. "He said, 'Immediately, right now. Take the tune out and get off the bandstand.'" And Ornette made the long walk back to Watts in the rain.

The California Club had jam sessions on Monday nights, and on one occasion, when Max Roach and Clifford Brown were in town, Ornette went down to sit in with them. He arrived in time for the first set, at about ten o'clock, but was told that he'd have to wait until later. They finally let him go up at about one forty-five—after Max and Clifford had finished their sets and had left the club. When he did get up on the bandstand, the entire rhythm section packed up their instruments and walked off. Blackwell and Cherry say that events like this were the rule rather than the exception for Ornette in those days.

Ornette finally did get a job at a Mexican place called Armand's, but it was back in his old Texas bag of accompanying dancers with the kind of gutsy rhythm-and-blues that he now knew by rote. He feels today that working that job was more frustrating than not working at all, for he had resolved that he would work in music only if the music he played was his own. Armand's was so discouraging for him that he quit and started searching out odd manual jobs to support his family. During this period he worked as a babysitter, a porter, an elevator operator, and a stock clerk. And he was fired consistently for studying music theory on the job. Don Cherry says that Ornette taught him an invaluable lesson during this period, that "no matter how much you get rejected, you put that much more study and work into it so that you can produce more."

Ornette began woodshedding* with a group of young musicians with whom he was in accord about the necessity for certain basic changes in approach to group and solo playing. The first group he practiced with included Blackwell and two Texas musicians, tenorman James Clay and trumpeter Bobby Bradford. Bradford had gotten Ornette the stockroom job, from which his take-home pay had been thirty-two dollars per week. Ornette still thinks that Bradford is "one of the best trumpet players alive. I've always wanted to keep him with me, but I couldn't afford to keep a band together when I wasn't working. I've had the publicity to do that, but I've never made the money." The group began to change when Clay had to go into the army (from which he

---

* "Woodshedding" is the musician's term for removing oneself from the scene to work on one's craft privately or with others.

emerged to join the Ray Charles orchestra), and Bradford soon followed him.

George Newman and Don Cherry were their replacements in the woodshed. Clay and Cherry had been working together around Los Angeles in a group called the Jazz Messiahs, and it was Clay who first took Cherry and Newman to Ornette's for rehearsal.

Cherry says that Ornette's main concern at the time was developing a distinctive sound. "As I remember, it was by his sound that I first recognized Ornette. I had known his wife, and she had been telling me about him, about how he sounded, but I had never heard or met him." Their first encounter took place in a Los Angeles record shop which specialized in stocking a selection of the best jazz releases. It was operated by a former jazz musician—a reed man—who also carried such jazz accessories as drumsticks, brushes, scores, and reeds. Ornette happened to be in the store trying out a thick number four and one-half reed as Cherry and Newman approached. They heard a sound with a brilliance they had never heard emanating from an alto saxophone before, and concluded that it must be Ornette Coleman. It was. Later on, in practice, Newman tried Ornette's horn and couldn't get a sound out of it. The reed was too thick and the mouthpiece too open, requiring an unusual amount of air. This itself is an example of the kind of discipline that Ornette had acquired during those months of not working in jazz. Because he had developed special muscles to control the wind, his neck swells outside the collar when he plays as it does with few reed men.

Cherry describes those sessions in George Newman's garage as purely cooperative efforts. There was a consistent exchange of ideas, and even of instruments. Cherry was only nineteen when he first started rehearsing with Ornette, and it was during those years that his ideas on music were shaped. He says: "I never had too much comment on music at that time since I was too young to have critical opinions. I thought that Ornette's music was a language that I didn't quite understand, but I think I could see the purity of it. Ornette and Blackwell got a short job at a beer tavern in midtown and I went there to hear them, and I was startled at the kind of unity that they could achieve. It had the jazz sounds and the jazz quality, but in terms of the kind of love and communication that they could achieve it had the quality of some African rhythms I've heard in which the communication is more important than the music, if you could separate the two. They had obviously developed the music together."

It is ironic that the only effect all this hard work had on Ornette's fellow musicians was to convince them that he didn't know his instrument, for his sound was different every time they heard it.

Cherry had come to Ornette with the long, convoluted arpeggios of Clifford Brown and the soft muted tones of Miles Davis. Unlike Ornette, at nineteen Don Cherry already had been popular with such Los Angeles musicians as Dexter Gordon and saxophonist Wardell Grey. He had been playing trumpet "almost from birth," and his zest for jazz had gotten him in trouble: "In Los Angeles there was a school that had a very good swing band. And there was a very good Negro teacher there named Daniel Brown. His band played things that Dizzy Gillespie played. He played piano. The school was Jefferson High School, and it was out of my district. I had heard the band playing some Stan Kenton things, some arrangements students had made, and some Dizzy Gillespie things, and I wanted to go to this school. Since I couldn't, I would ditch my sixth-period class and go to their rehearsals. I told Mr. Brown that I was in Jefferson High School. He kept me in the band, because, like, I could solo too. We would go to other schools to play concerts. This finally got me into so much trouble at my own school that they kicked me out and sent me to a detention school. I started a small band there, even though they had very few instruments, because it was, like, a very poor school. Billy Higgins came in to play drums in this band. I had only known him from seeing him around. So when I would call the rehearsals, Billy wouldn't show up half the time because he'd be out playing basketball or something. I told him that he should be more serious about his music because he had a lot of talent.

"By being good at the detention school I got to go to the school I wanted to when I left. After I finished high school, Billy and I got some jobs together playing shuffle piano and drums in a rhythm-and-blues group."

Don brought Billy to George Newman's, where Billy joined the woodshedding group. Meeting Blackwell was a revelation for Billy Higgins. When he first saw Blackwell, Blackwell had a set of drums he had made himself that looked like a toy set. Don said, "We couldn't figure out at first what he was doing, though we knew it was different and we knew it was real." Blackwell had done a lot of studying, both of traditional New Orleans drums when he had lived there, and of African and Bata (Afro-Cuban) drumming, and he had brought all of this study to his own style of playing. He has a reverential approach to drums, and building his own set is typical of him, concerned as he is with knowing every aspect of percussion. Blackwell, always a superior technician, became Higgins' tutor, conscientiously involved in bringing the talent that he recognized out from under the convention-minded clichés of the teen-age drummer. Blackwell taught Higgins the responsibility of the drummer, and the importance of technique. He had cultivated the New

Orleans march sound so that he was able to impart that pedestrian quality (in the nonpejorative sense) to the modern sound. With Blackwell's technique and with his knowledge of the sonics of drums, he was able to play overtones that few drummers were aware of, and this knowledge too he imparted to Higgins.

Although Ornette's music had not brought him any closer to acceptance by the rest of the musicians with whom he had to deal, one important difference now was that when he went to sit in at the various clubs, he didn't have to go up alone. Bassist Don Payne and pianist Walter Norris had joined the group, and now they could go up as a unit. Don says: "At first he had to be by himself, but when we went with him we showed that it was possible for somebody else to play his music. It's the same as when Albert Ayler [an important new tenor saxophonist] went to Europe: He was by himself, and people thought it was the only way you could play that music, by yourself. But then he ran into Cecil Taylor and people saw that it was possible for this music to happen with two people. It's beautiful either way, but we all feel it's better if it can happen with more people."

Ornette felt that even if he couldn't get gigs in the clubs, he was ready for a record. Newman had been working with bassist Red Mitchell earlier and had introduced Ornette to Mitchell. Red Mitchell had a good reputation in the jazz business and was always near the top of the jazz polls in the late Fifties. Newman thought that Mitchell might introduce Ornette and his music to the company that recorded him, Contemporary, a Los Angeles label directed by Lester Koenig. A session was arranged at Don Payne's house where Mitchell was to listen to Ornette's music and give his objective opinion about its salability. Mitchell rendered a judgment that was to plague Ornette for years to come: that he was better as a composer than as an improviser and that his tunes were more marketable than his playing. That judgment was rendered in more diplomatic terms, but this was nonetheless the conclusion, and was the only term under which Mitchell would lend his name to a meeting of Ornette and Koenig.

Ornette then went to the Contemporary studios, introduced himself to Koenig, using Mitchell's name, and sat down at the piano to try to sell Koenig some of his tunes. But he could only play a composer's piano—could only finger out the tunes and the chords he had in mind, without being able to play them in any relaxed, interpretive way. For Koenig, who was listening for music that he might be able to use for some pick-up groups he might record, the beginning of that session was more confusing than enlightening, and was leading nowhere. Fortunately, Ornette had brought his plastic alto saxophone with him, and Don Cherry had come along to lend moral support. They gave up on the piano, and Coleman and Cherry played the tunes *a cappella;* Koenig was sufficiently impressed to offer Ornette a recording date.

Ornette and Cherry went out and organized their woodshed group to record the tunes they had been rehearsing all along. (It is an interesting sidelight that everyone in this band, with the exception of Billy Higgins, is from the South and Southwest. The pianist on this first date was Walter Norris, a Little Rock, Arkansas, musician. Don Cherry had grown up in Los Angeles but was born in Oklahoma City. And Don Payne, who, like Cherry, had grown up in Los Angeles, was born in Wellington, Texas. Ed Blackwell would have made the date, but he had returned to New Orleans by that time.) *Something Else! The Music of Ornette Coleman,* was a far more prophetic record than its reviewers could have realized. Nat Hentoff, who wrote some unusually acute and honest liner notes for it, provided a good analysis of the tunes and did a good job of selecting self-descriptive quotes by Ornette, but he did not try to make a case for Ornette and the rest of the group as innovators. Listening to the record now, one can see why: Everything was there, the angular melodic lines, the compressed emotionalism, the intergroup exchanges, but they had not become the actual format of the group as they were to be a year later. Don Payne, the bassist on *Something Else!*, is strong and correct, but he did not have the constant assertion of Charlie Haden, who was to become the group's bassist within the next few months. And Ornette was soon to stop using a pianist altogether, thus dispersing the chord center throughout the group.

I might say at this point that my own response to *Something Else!* at the time was typical of the general critical response. I recall that when I first heard the record in 1958, I thought the saxophonist was some oddball imitator of Charlie Parker. But I can see now that this was more because of the rhythmic placement of his notes than because of the actual melodic material that he was using. On first hearing, I actually did not recognize the melodic content of Ornette's music at all, and I have since learned from talking to some others who have not been able to understand Ornette's music, that these melodies, simple as they are, are difficult to sort out if one is offended by the sound of Ornette's instrument.

Don Cherry was even more difficult to hear, because in 1958 I was accustomed to the well-clipped arpeggios of the hard-boppers—Clifford Brown and his followers. Cherry's notes, like Ornette's, seemed imprecise, accidentally arrived at. He was working on a kind of construction of his solos that was not at all like the glibness I was accustomed to during

the Fifties. What was immediately obvious was the originality of the tunes. "The Invisible," "The Disguise," and "The
Chippie" were obviously compositions of exceptional originality, of the kind I had not heard since Charlie Parker's
and Dizzy Gillespie's early fertile days, and in that my
opinion was not unlike Mitchell's. In listening to any recording by a "new" musician, one must take into account that the
record companies are forever finding "geniuses" who make a
couple of records, a little bit of noise, and disappear, so that
one listens with perhaps too many grains of salt, assumes that
a musician whose work has not been heard in progress over
a period of years will be poor. (This is an unfortunate and
even dangerous assumption, but one that the ear gets jaded
into. John Coltrane, for example, has been recognized as a
truly new voice on saxophone ever since his tenure with
Thelonious Monk; but Coltrane had come up through the
ranks, unlike Coleman and Cecil Taylor, who had always
been outsiders, and his music was showcased in the most
respectable band then going—the Miles Davis group—before he became a leader.)

However, even a closer reading of the liner notes of
Something Else! might have indicated that we were listening to something that deserved very close scrutiny. The
quotations from the musicians indicated that a truly new
music was being worked at by these men: Walter Norris'
comment that "each time we played the tunes we changed
them around a different way. We did everything possible we
could do with them" is definitely not the attitude that was
taken in the hard-bop groups. Horace Silver and Art Blakey
kept their repertoire as familiar as possible, keeping the fans
happy, but following a formula that was certain to stagnate
their groups. In 1958, you could tell what a new tune played

by the Jazz Messengers or the Horace Silver group would sound like before you heard it.

Cherry had said of Ornette in the jacket notes that "he uses a plastic alto; it has a drier warmer sound without the ping of the metal. He also has a special mouthpiece that together with the number-one reed he uses has enabled him to develop his tone so that he can control it. He has real control of pitch, and the pitch is so important to him. He can now express on his horn what he hears, and he has a very unusual ear." If one had turned his ear to *Something Else!* in search of just what it was that Cherry was talking about, one might have been able to take this record more literally, and uncovered the melodic values there. Likewise, Ornette's comment about sounds and chords was more of a key to what was to happen in the future than to what actually occurred on this record. "There are some intervals that carry that *human* quality if you play them in the right pitch. I don't care how many intervals a person can play on an instrument; you can always reach into the human sound of a voice on your horn if you're actually hearing and trying to express the warmth of the human voice. I always write the melody line first because several different chords can fit the same melody line. In fact, I would prefer it if musicians would play my tunes with different changes as they take a new chorus so that there'd be more variety in the performance. On this recording the changes finally decided on for the tunes are a combination of some I suggested and some the musicians suggested. If you feel the lines different one day, you can change the harmony accordingly."

All of which indicates, as Quincy Jones observed in the *Jazz Review,* that the piano would soon be eliminated from future Coleman groups to enhance the aleatory character of the music. Most important were the rhythmic ideas that

Ornette had hoped to put into practice and which were later to become the main basis of his contribution to group playing: "Rhythm patterns should be more or less like natural breathing patterns. I would like the rhythm section to be as free as I'm trying to get, but very few players, rhythm or horns, can do this yet. Thelonious Monk can. He sometimes plays one note, and because he plays it in exactly the right pitch, he carries more music in it than if he had filled out the chord. I'd say Monk has the most complete harmonic ear in jazz. Bird has the best diatonic ear. Monk can also play different rhythm patterns, and a drummer I know, Edward Blackwell, is another musician who can play all kinds of time."

Higgins had not developed the facility to shift from meter to meter in a given tune, a style of which he was later to become perhaps the principal spokesman. But it was all there in kernel. *Something Else!* fits now very comfortably into the body of Ornette's recorded jazz.

Six months before that record date, Ornette had been ready to go back to Fort Worth, perhaps to scrap his career altogether. It was all too discouraging. He was already having marital troubles, and his good friend George Newman, who had developed severe emotional problems, could no longer play with him. Los Angeles had been almost totally hostile to him, and there was no reason to think that New York might be better. His only encouragement was that he had found a small group of young but obviously talented musicians who were interested in the kind of music he was working on.

Now, however, in the weeks just prior to the *Something Else!* date, a few things began to fall his way. One gig was at the Club Malamo with Cherry and Clay. Another was Cherry's gig for a jazz society in Vancouver. That one included Ben Tucker and the modern pianist Don Friedman. Cherry stayed in Vancouver for some four months, figuring that he could work his way from there to New York, until Ornette wrote him about a record session. Cherry recalls that during one set at the Malamo they were playing "The Song Is You," and that while he was playing his solo, Ornette "whispered in my ear and told me about playing a flatted ninth from a flatted fifth and that put me a half step above the key I was playing in. Then I discovered another brilliance in music and it was a brilliancy that he had already discovered and gone beyond. That's when I learned that a musician gets brighter and brighter in tone as he goes along."

The first record had very little commercial success; though the reviews were favorable, it attracted little attention. For the second date then, Koenig decided to use Red Mitchell and Shelley Manne, by no means an important musician but, judging by his position near the top of most of the jazz polls of the last fifteen years, perhaps the most popular, if not the richest, drummer in the history of jazz. Manne reacted to the sessions with enthusiasm, telling Nat Hentoff, "I don't feel I'm actually playing a song. I'm really playing *with* a person. I'm playing *his* song. . . . Ornette does something with his own tunes that makes you not only hear the tunes but makes you hear them like 18,000,000 different ways!" Don and Ornette agree that Manne tried to meet the spirit of the group and provided a kind of alertness to the session, even though he didn't really understand the music.

Mitchell was somewhat recalcitrant, and seemed unable to bend to the demands of playing a music that was not designed to conform to a steady four/four or three/four beat. He did not play badly, but Ornette required a kind of playing Mitchell was unaccustomed to. Ornette said, "He really thought I was just out of my skull or something." That second record, *Tomorrow Is the Question,* was to be recorded in two dates; and Ornette and Don took the money they had made from the first date and went up to San Francisco in the wild hope that they could get Modern Jazz Quartet bassist Percy Heath to join them for the second date. There, they sat in with the Modern Jazz Quartet; this occasion was MJQ leader John Lewis' first introduction to their music. Lewis was more than impressed, and it was this first session with Don and Ornette that formed his lasting impression of them. He told Ornette that "if I didn't find anybody, then I should wait and talk to his man."

Heath came down to Los Angeles to make six tunes for *Tomorrow Is the Question.* With all the seeming rigidity of its musical organization, the Modern Jazz Quartet had used quite a few more musical devices than had most groups, so that Heath, his strong and steady metric accuracy notwithstanding, was better able than Mitchell to handle the odd breaks and releases which were the keynotes of Ornette's group concept. The over-all result was a record that showed Ornette to be a composer who was able to apply a kind of group construction that would obviously affect the course of coming jazz, even though one half of his group was new to the music and therefore unable to contribute the kind of exact meandering it required. *Tomorrow Is the Question* caught Cherry and Coleman, as soloists, in a much more assertive mood than before, and it is difficult to see why anyone whose mind was not entirely closed to this music could have failed to recognize their originality and vitality as soloists.

Tomorrow Is the Question was edited at Lenox, Massachusetts, and issued just prior to Ornette's opening at the Five Spot. Nat Hentoff again wrote the liner notes, and it is interesting to note the change of attitude that had taken place in the interval. His notes open: "I am especially convinced that Ornette Coleman is making an unique and valuable contribution to 'tomorrow's' music because of the startling power of his playing to reach the most basic emotions." The sides were lining up, and Hentoff was making a strong assertion of what side he was on.

Between the two record sessions, Ornette had only one job. It was at the Hilcrest Club, in a mixed neighborhood on the West Side of Los Angeles, and lasted about six weeks. The Hilcrest Club was an important one during its time for Los Angeles musicians, for it hired local talent exclusively.

The job at the Hilcrest was with pianist Paul Bley, and it was the last that Ornette was to take as a sideman. The group included Billy Higgins, Don Cherry, Ornette, Bley, and bassist Charlie Haden—a momentous development for Ornette, because he found in Haden the bassist he had been looking for. Ornette says that Haden made tremendous progress during this period at the Hilcrest, where he largely developed his style of playing. A few years later his method of juxtaposing independent bass lines against the lines of the soloist was hailed as a milestone in group playing. Two things impressed Ornette about Haden: that he had that peculiar ear Ornette has always been on the lookout for in musicians, and that he was ready to listen to Ornette's suggestions about the bassist's responsibility in the group. Ornette explained to him his aleatory conception of bass accompaniment: "Forget about the changes in key and just play within the range of the idea. If I'm in the high register just play within that range that fits that register and just play the bass, that's all, all you've got to do is play the bass. So he tried and he would have a difficult problem of knowing which range I was playing in and just what I meant by the whole range of playing anyway. I told him, 'Well, just learn.' So after a while of playing with me it just became the natural thing for him to do. All that matters in the function of the bass is either the top or the bottom or the middle, that's all the bass player has to play for me. It doesn't mean because you put an F7 down for the bass player he's going to choose the best notes in the F7 to express what you're doing. But if he's allowed to use any note that he hears to express that F7, then that note's going to be right because he hears it, not because he read it off the page. I've had a problem with bass players and I have had some good ones, but I think Charlie is the closest I've been, of all the guys that have been with me."

This, then, was the group that Ornette brought to New York in the fall of 1959. Don Cherry, Charlie Haden, and Billy Higgins, all barely out of their teens, and Ornette himself, then twenty-nine. Everyone who talked to Ornette during this time attests to his modesty, if not his outright humility. I think *gentle* was the word most often used. Again, the opinions were either virulently for or against him; there was no middle ground. The Five Spot flourished; controversy is one of the oldest and most reliable of attention-getters.

Everything about this group was striking: its funny little waistcoats, which Ornette himself had designed, the white plastic alto saxophone of the leader, and the miniature pocket trumpet ("by its being this short it enables you to hear yourself back") which Don Cherry played, even the way the men approached each other on the stand. Each man, furthermore, had his own mannerisms. Drummers tend to grimace as if in agony, but Billy Higgins kept a silly little grin on his face, as if his drums were telling jokes to the rest of the band. Charlie Haden would bend himself around the bass until his head was almost at the bottom of its bridge. Don Cherry, thin and big-headed, had cheeks that swelled out like balloons as he played, seemingly to his image, which faced him in the mirror behind the bar. And then there was Ornette, practically biting his horn and fighting with the music, as if in a rage. Obviously, there was something *to* this music, although not everyone knew what.

Compared to the kind of adversity described in the preceding pages, Ornette's first year in New York must be considered a success. Within eighteen months of his opening at the Five Spot, at least a dozen articles had been written about him, four of his LP's had been released, and several others were "in the can." He certainly had his detractors, but he was used to that by now. His supporters, although probably not so numerous as his detractors, were fanatical, and of sufficient number to assure him a paying audience.

Within two years, Ornette's work had had a profound effect on the two most influential reedmen of the Fifties— John Coltrane and, indirectly, Sonny Rollins. Coltrane came to hear Ornette whenever he was in New York, and admits not only that Ornette showed him an entirely new range of possibilities for his own playing but also that his own music entered a new phase of improvisation with a good deal more abandon than he had allowed before listening to Ornette.

Sonny Rollins, on the other hand, withdrew from the jazz scene for two years. Rollins has explained that it was for personal reasons that he would not play in public, that the strains of handling the financial and personal needs of a group night after night, week after week, and year after year, had taken all the joy out of playing. This is probably true, but it is also true that Rollins, in a musical sense, was caught off guard by the "free" jazz of Ornette Coleman and the all-out, unrestricted confessional soloing of John Coltrane. These two reedmen, along with pianist Cecil Taylor, had taken jazz to a new level of expression whose premises and demands were as radical as those of Charlie Parker's and Dizzy Gillespie's had been back in the Forties. Rollins' tenor style had been the embodiment of the deep-voiced tenor style of the Fifties (what might be called "uncool"), but it had not broadened to meet the new vitality of the music of the Sixties. It is fair to say that when Rollins came out of the woodshed, people went to hear his first performances and bought his first two LP's to see just how he was to handle the music that Coleman, Coltrane, and Taylor had proposed. Those first LP's and club engagements showed Rollins playing the same music that he had retired with. Then he opened at the Village Gate with two of Ornette's prodigies, Billy Higgins and Don Cherry, and fell, to the horror of the conservatives who had always applauded Rollins as their hope for tradition, into the "New Thing."

It is worthwhile to note here parenthetically that Coleman, Taylor, and Coltrane are working on entirely different, though interrelated, principles. Coleman's main contribution to jazz may be said to be rhythmic, even though there has been considerable discussion of his tonality. Coltrane's is harmonic, setting, as he does, his wildest explorations against definite chordal patterns. Taylor is involved with the construction and the organization of sound. Some of the musicians who have followed these men are putting all these innovations together, as is natural, but the breakthroughs have been by these three.

The late reedman Eric Dolphy is another musician who admittedly benefited from the work of these three men. Dolphy's work sounded closer to Coltrane's than to Coleman's, as he was not the melodist Ornette is. His group concept, however, as evidenced by his last American record

(*Out to Lunch* on Blue Note label), was more like Coleman's.

By 1962 there were beginning to appear in New York a few new reedmen who were directly or indirectly influenced by Ornette Coleman. There was the flutist Prince Lasha from Ornette's home town, who was writing compositions that sounded like Ornette's earlier work. Sonny Simmons was playing a plastic alto saxophone, and his solos were largely indistinguishable from Ornette Coleman's. John Tchichai, a Danish Negro, was appearing at loft concerts and sometimes playing Ornette Coleman licks almost verbatim. (Today Tchichai resents having people refer to an Ornette Coleman influence in his playing. But at that time the influence was clear.) Even such an old head as Jackie McLean had dipped into Ornette's methodology to broaden his own work, and the eclectic saxophonist Roland Kirk included Ornette Coleman innovations in his act.

The effect of Ornette's group sound was more immediate than that of his compositions or his soloing. The original Ornette Coleman quartet at the Five Spot emancipated bass players and drummers more than it did saxophonists and trumpeters. Leaders and section men realized that it was no longer necessary to have the bassist and the drummers function as metronomes, waiting for their solo break or for the four coda with the lead instruments to make a statement on their own. Higgins and Haden (and later Scott LaFaro and Blackwell, and Jimmy Garrison or David Izenzon and Moffett) played rhythms that ran counter to the horn lines and usually brought in extracompositional materials. The drum and the bass were liberated from the function of accompanying, and the gap between rhythm and solo was greatly reduced, if not eliminated altogether. Given this new freedom and responsibility, bassists seemed almost overnight to develop new technical facilities, and bassists who could play their instruments like saxophones proliferated.

Ornette further developed the pianoless group, which had been an innovation of Gerry Mulligan's back in the early Fifties. Now that there was no need for the chord changes to be laid out for the other instruments to follow, the piano was no longer a necessary staple of the rhythm section, much to the benefit of the concept of free improvisation.

Ornette's first year and a half after Lenox included six months at the Five Spot, a four- or five-month tour of the Midwest and West, and then another six-month stand at the Five Spot. Meanwhile, he had enjoyed a prominent place ("some felt too prominent," wrote a *Down Beat* critic) at the Monterey Jazz Festival. He had also acquired an in with some of the leading artistic figures of the day, and men of the stature of artist Larry Rivers and conductor Leonard Bernstein claimed Ornette as one of their own, though he says, "I never asked to be adopted." Bernstein sat in with Ornette once, and one of the sidemen present at that intrusion remembers: "He didn't really know anything about what was going on." Even Miles Davis sat in with Ornette, and students of modern jazz personalities will know what a rare event *that* is.

Nonetheless, Ornette was soon disillusioned. There were things he had expected from success that simply turned out to have been the illusions of a Texas boy. The most outstanding area of his disillusionment was in the lingering, undefined racism that black people experience in superliberal New York. He was not being called a nigger, as he had been in Texas, nor being arbitrarily stopped on the street and searched by policemen, as he had been in Los Angeles. Nor was it anything as obvious as the fact that cabs ignored him, or that he could not rent the apartment he wanted. It had more to do with the fact that Ornette had viewed success as a situation in which he could assemble some men who had a common outlook on their work, prove their worth, and then have jobs (as a musical outlet) fall naturally into place. But New York is a hustler's town: cabs and apartments, openings in nightclubs, as well as record contracts are fought for, and honesty is a useless weapon. "I haven't had any more success in New York City in relation to musical expression than I had anywhere else. New York City has prejudice embedded in wealth as well as color. Wealth is first and color is next; in California color is first and wealth is next. All the musical life in New York is determined by the money output that it can produce. I'm like a lot of other people who come here thinking that they're going to find their fame and fortune and find out that all they're doing is supporting a lot of unsuccessful people and giving wealth to a lot of untalented people."

Ornette made eight more records, a total (at this writing) of ten, but as yet he says he has never received a royalty check large enough to pay his phone bill. In fact, one company informed him in 1965 that he owed *them* money. The musician is defenseless in the area of royalties on record sales, with no access to the companies' books; but Ornette does not feel that he would have been recorded as often as he has nor publicized as much if his music were not salable. A reputable critic has said that one record of Ornette's was reissued three times, and had a gross sale of 25,000 copies. If this is so, and if he received no royalties, it would be a clear case of fraud. Ornette described the situation himself: "I've had record companies record me, I've had publicity written about me, and I've had musicians and other people admire me; but according to my production output, I haven't earned anything. The problem is in this business that you don't own your own product. If you record, it's the record company that owns it; if you play at a club, it's the nightclub owners who charge people to listen to you, and then they tell you your music is not catching on. Let's say I've made eight albums; if one company owns six of them and the other owns two, then who do you think made the most money from them? Me or the two companies? Maybe that's what business is, taking something and making money from it. But the thing that gets me is that they say I'm so far out that people haven't caught on.

"It seems that production and publicity are so closely related that they turn into the same thing. What I mean is, in jazz the Negro is the product. The way they handle the publicity on me, about how far out I am and everything, it gets to be that I'm the product myself. So if it's me they're selling, if I'm the product, then the profits couldn't come back to me, you dig? I don't know what percentage Negroes make from jazz, but I know it's got to be very small.

"This has been my greatest problem—being short-changed because I'm a Negro, not because I can't produce. Here I am being used as a Negro who can play jazz, and all the people I recorded for and worked for act as if they own me and my product. They have been guilty of making me believe I shouldn't have the profits from my product simply because they own the channels of production. They say, 'Here is a guy who can play off the top of his head and he's not a part of the structure, so we'll take it and use it for our own betterment and let him feel that he's just becoming a human being, you know, expressing himself.' They act like I owe them something for letting me express myself with my music, like the artist is supposed to suffer and not to live in clean, comfortable situations.

"This is the worst kind of suffering. This psychological

suffering of knowing that you're being exploited, whether it's whites doing it to whites or whites doing it to blacks or blacks doing it to blacks, it's still the same thing. But I'll tell you this, I'm thirty-five years old, and I don't believe I'll live to see the time when blacks will be exploiting whites.

"The insanity of living in America is that ownership is really strength. It's who owns who's strongest in America. It's strategic living. That's why it's so hard to lend your music to that kind of existence."

Ornette's salary scale has been much lower than that of other musicians who are even less prestigious. He opened at the Five Spot at four hundred dollars per week for the entire group: "I've never gotten $2,000 a week yet. The most I've gotten is $1,200 a week. And yet I've packed audiences into the same clubs that have been paying $4,000 a week to people who haven't packed the house. I was pulling packed houses in one club with $1,200 a week, and then they brought Dave Brubeck in the next week and paid him several times that amount, and he didn't fill the house at all. In fact they lost money on Dave Brubeck. So if I'm packing the house and making as much money for the man as people who are getting paid more than me, then wouldn't it seem that I should get the same amount?"

Ornette had never worked enough in Los Angeles or Texas to have the problem of keeping a group together for prolonged periods of time. Leading a band entails a different kind of responsibility than most artists are accustomed to, involving as it does several other sensibilities than the bandleader's. The leader must see to it that his band members show up in time for every set of every gig, prepared and equipped, and he must make certain that the group is not shortchanged by its employers. Yet almost every aspect of the unfortunate social life that jazz has fallen heir to pressures the jazz musicians to satisfy their most irresponsible needs first. They are employed by bartender types who treat them as disrespectfully as they treat waiters, cooks, and busboys, so that all the years of study and hard work that would give status to performing artists in other fields mean nothing in jazz. To hold on to their self-respect, musicians must keep reminding themselves that it is they who support the employer, not the other way around.

There is also the underground aspect of jazz: The music is played primarily in bars, and the musicians work bar hours, seldom leaving their jobs earlier than four o'clock in the morning. This means that the jazz musicians' associates become the types that frequent bars, a variegated group indeed. Many bar owners pay their musicians in alcohol, so that the performers run up large tabs, which at the end of the week absorb a good percent of their salary. And there are always women in the bars who consider it a status symbol to have a musician in their beds.

These are diversions that the musician may use to whatever extent he chooses. Women do not break up bands, and I have met fewer jazz musicians who could not handle their liquor than I have business executives. Addictive drugs are another matter. Probably no more than five or so percent of all jazz musicians are heroin addicts, but the opportunities for addiction are easily found. Most jazz musicians know drug dealers, and all know addicts. A man susceptible to heroin addiction can have all the opportunity he likes to pick up on it in the jazz scene. Addiction does sometimes beget addiction, and I have known of at least one major quintet that was, a few years ago, composed entirely of addicts (the leader still leads a band under the same name, but the personnel has changed, and he himself is no longer addicted).

Ornette Coleman does not use addictive drugs, but at

times he has had to work with bands in which the majority of the musicians were addicts. At these times Ornette's sidemen sometimes appeared for work without their instruments, which were in the pawnshop; on some occasions, if their habit called, they did not show up at all. Thus Ornette, the leader and nonuser, would have to dig into his pocket for loans for his sidemen, with a resultant strain on personal relationships, as such loans soon become abusive. Because these men were all friends and had invested a great deal of time with one another in the development of their music, it was impossible for Ornette to maintain simple attitudes toward the problems of his cohorts. Sometimes, when the group was out of work, Ornette had to approach the record companies to beg for recording dates to make a payday for the group so that his musicians could support their habits. One man, arrested out of the state for possession of narcotics, had his police-department cabaret card rescinded in New York City, so that he was unable to work at all.

Why so many members of Ornette Coleman's band, or of any bands, used heroin at one time, I cannot say. I have known several people from various backgrounds who have come to New York and encountered a kind of pressure and pace that was altogether different from what they were accustomed to, and who have literally died from the weight of it. It may be this same combination of pressures that pushes so many New Yorkers, particularly black New Yorkers, into drugs, but whatever the reasons, the drug scene in New York City is larger and more destructive than anywhere else in the world.

At any rate, leading a group in New York was for Ornette a wearying proposition, for he did not have the business experience that it takes to be a financially successful leader.

He had led three groups, all with generally the same critical and popular response: the first with Billy Higgins, Charlie Haden, and Don Cherry; the second with Ed Blackwell, Charlie Haden (later Scott LaFaro), and Don Cherry; the third with Charlie Moffett, Jimmy Garrison (later replaced by Ornette's current bassist, David Izenzon), and Bobby Bradford. Bradford had been unable to face a long period of unemployment that was imminent after Ornette's last Five Spot engagement in 1962, and returned to Texas; he has never been heard from since. It was a great disappointment for Ornette, who said, "I think Bobby Bradford is one of the best trumpet players alive," and some jazz critics, notably LeRoi Jones, had proclaimed Bradford a coming force on his instrument. Later, Ornette took a trio into the Jazz Gallery, where he drew his ever-growing audience almost nightly. It was here that his bitterness for the scene hardened after seeing Dave Brubeck follow him into the club and earn many times the money Ornette's group had. Ornette tripled his pay demands for nightclub appearances, on the basis that he should be paid according to the house that he drew. These demands were immediately rejected by the nightclub owners, and horrified Ornette's personal agent. Suddenly, record dates and concert engagements disappeared. His sidemen became disgruntled by the lack of work, but they bore it. When Charlie Moffett saw what was coming he took a job teaching school in New York City. (He had been one of the leading bandleaders in the Texas high school system.) David Izenzon looked around for double-bass jobs in chamber groups and symphony orchestras.

In the winter of 1962, Ornette rented Town Hall for a concert that was to be his swan song for the next three years. He used two supplementary groups for this evening, one a rhythm-and-blues group, and the other a string quartet. The concert consisted of trio pieces for the Ornette Coleman group, a combined work for rhythm-and-blues and jazz trio, and a string quartet. The string quartet, on analysis, could only have been written by Ornette Coleman; but, on hearing, it sounds nothing like anything Ornette's music would suggest. This is perhaps due to the fact that Ornette's music depends so much on his persona. Though his compositions could be played by almost any competent jazz group open to the ideas proposed therein, Ornette writes for himself. His writing is directed toward setting up areas of improvisational possibilities, and not toward strict interpretation. His music is the antithesis of such interpretation. The string quartet, therefore, was not, by Ornette's own standards, successful. The musicians, three of whom were Negro, did not understand it.

The piece for combined instrumental rhythm-and-blues group and the Ornette Coleman trio was considerably more successful because Ornette played during its entire course and thereby assumed the role of conductor. That piece must stand, with Ornette Coleman's record *Free Jazz,* as one of the two most important works that he has ever performed. So much occurred in the interplay of the strict rhythm-and-blues beat of the trio and the polyrhythmic playing of Charlie Moffett and David Izenzon that one wonders why all other jazzmen concerned with enlarging their forms did not stop and re-evaluate their music. Ornette's solo included everything that he had learned since his early Texas days. His use of those old rhythm-and-blues licks was conscious, and it was his concern in this work to solo just high enough above the two groups to include the demands of both in his playing. The piece was embarrassing in its honesty. It was as if Ornette had excavated his entire musical past to get back to the core of his work. There was something intensely autobiographical about this particular piece which one cannot define but can simply point to. It seemed to include all those things that a man hesitates to say about himself.

This concert, which broke even—he was able to pay the musicians, but did not realize a profit—was the end of Ornette's musical presence for two years. Club owners, record companies, and producers of concerts would not meet his price, and he would not lower it to meet their offers. His was not an objective decision to stop playing in public until certain adjustments were made, as Sonny Rollins' had been; it was more an accident of the market. Ornette's listeners numbered far more than ever before, and they were confused as to why their hero was not appearing in the clubs. They did not understand his motives for this self-removal; most of them thought he should take whatever he could get while he waited for conditions to improve.

Moffett took a couple of jobs in jazz coffee shops and made some loft concerts, but he relied mostly on his school-teaching salary to get him and his growing family through the hiatus. Izenzon took work in chamber groups and symphony orchestras, and had one nightclub engagement with pianist Joe Sciani; but like Moffett, Izenzon was marking time until the leader chose to come out of retirement at whatever wage.

Offers were being made for Ornette now, but they did not meet his minimum salary requirement, and he rejected them all. Intermittently, he felt ready to play for almost any wage, but on these occasions he could not find a club owner who would hire him even at prices lower than those they had offered him before. Izenzon recalls, "It seems that when Ornette wanted to play, they wouldn't hire him; and when they would hire him, he didn't want to play." Except that Ornette *did* want to play through this entire period.

The problem was that Ornette had lost confidence in the jazz scene, in the possibilities of making a living at an equitable wage in jazz. He thought that he might ameliorate the situation by taking matters into his control as he had attempted to do with the concert. He decided to open his own nightclub, liquorless if necessary, and thus escape the exploitation of club owners who were committed to profit and not to music. He would pay the musicians according to the audience they drew, and payment would be prorated on the basis of the net profit. The problem was, as David Izenzon said, "Ornette is just not a businessman. He just does not have a good business sense to know when things are working to his advantage and when things are working against him." Ornette rented a room large enough for a fair-sized jazz club, but that was as far as he got before he was confronted with licensing and zoning laws. The club was closed before it could be decorated, because it was situated in an area zoned as residential, a fact about which the landlord had never bothered to inform Ornette. He wound up being billed for alterations that were never made as well as for the terms of the lease.

The same kind of trouble befell Ornette's publishing company. He planned a company that would be equitable in dealing with the problems of musicians, who composed tunes that were used and reused, sometimes under a very superficial disguise, without compensation. Again, the result was zero; today he owns a publishing company on paper, but not in fact.

Ornette used that two-year interval when he was not playing for reflection, for further composition, and for study of other instruments. He also reviewed such problems as drugs in his group: "One of the things that I've come to learn about narcotics is that everybody expects the musician in some way to be just naturally out of his mind, whatever it is. I mean some people say, 'Well man, you might not smoke or drink or nothing, but music is your high.' You know. Even if you haven't had nothing, not even a drink of water, they'd say, 'Well, baby, you know, even if you ain't high on nothing, just that shit you're playing is high.'

"But I don't have any moral thing against drugs, you know. I've had the LSD experience several times, for example. But I've never used anything, drugs or liquor or anything, to keep my emotions up so that I can express myself. Real individual self-expression is so rare, so rare, that when the person uses any kind of stimulant to maintain his emotional energy, it always works against his expression. He usually tends to have to socialize with people that are not really out of his bag, you know, in expression, but who see him as having the same problem. The guys who used drugs in my band, they would be dealing with people that would steal from you or beat you out of anything, and all these people had in common was just that they needed to get high. It wasn't to elevate their minds to play better music. It makes a situation that takes up a lot of your emotional energy and can only hurt your playing.

"Like, I don't care if the person is using LSD, heroin, marijuana, whiskey, and sex all in the same day, if it helps him get up and do something that he truly believes in. To me if such a person can obtain that kind of energy and individual style without any harm done to himself, then more power to him."

Another observation that Ornette made from his experiences on the bandstand—one that I've heard confirmed by several other jazz musicians—is that the relationship between the performer and the audience is largely sexual: "Jazz musicians also get a screwed-up sex life, and that sucks up a lot of their energy. When the musician goes out and plays for the public on a bandstand, ninety percent of his audience in the nightclub is sexually oriented, you know, basically. Ninety percent of them. It's like the guy will sit there, and if they're really digging you, he'll start feeling the girl, you know. Or if the girl digs you, he gets up and takes her away. So therefore, it ain't music. It's sexual attraction. And then when the musician gets this idea, the first thing he's going to do is he's going to forget what he's up there for and he's going to start saying, 'Wait, man, where'd that bitch go that I had my eye on when I was cooking?' You don't know how many times I've come off the bandstand and had girls come up to me and hand me a note with their address on it. And all those other things. Sometimes I say to myself, 'Well, shit, if this is what it's all about, we should all be standing up there with hard-ons, and everybody should come to the club naked, and the musicians should be standing up there naked. Then there wouldn't be any confusion about what's supposed to happen, and people wouldn't say they came to hear the music.' I'm telling you, the whole sex thing has more of a negative effect on the music than drugs, I'm sure of it. So you see, the jazz scene hasn't really changed that much since it left the New Orleans whorehouses. The nightclub is still built on the same two things: whiskey and fucking."

It has been reported that the Budapest String Quartet stayed together for decades by avoiding all social relationships with one another outside of the rehearsal room and the concert hall. Jazz musicians, of course, are forced, by the nature of their society and their music, into very close social relationships, and such an arrangement as the Budapest's is out of the question within a jazz group. Yet it would seem that

New York, with all its pressures, made impossible the intimate intergroup relationship that Ornette had enjoyed with the sidemen he had known since his Texas and Los Angeles days: "I guess it was a matter of ambitions. When the cats came to New York they became ability-conscious from seeing the kind of public reaction they could get and the kind of musical importance the magazines were saying we all had. They all started feeling that they were indispensable. They started giving me the feeling that they were indispensable, and I had to pay. Up until then I had respect and I was giving them what I thought was fair and they trusted me, because they had a certain kind of respect for what I was trying to do. After we got to New York, money got to be a big thing with us, and the guys started making demands. I started feeling that if that was the case after we got to New York, then it must have been the case all along, only it had not been brought out in the clear. I was never conscious of any feeling like this with sidemen before, but ever since I've been in New York I've never been able to get rid of it."

One thing that has always been in the air but never stated in Ornette's group has been the matter of the white bass player. If a group is all black or all white, the question of race can never impede its development. But if the group is racially mixed, its musicians invariably take a position, tacit perhaps, about the mixed group, and this attitude may well intrude into the music at certain points. Of the nine musicians who have worked with Ornette for any length of time, three have been white, and each of those three was a bassist. Could such a thing be coincidental? Ornette found it a long and complex matter for which he had no single analysis. Yes, he had noticed that some white bass players he had found satisfied the needs of his group better than their black counterparts. As this question related to so much of

Ornette's vision of music and the world, it is recorded here in all the length he used to explain it: "If there was a white bass player who was really a bitch and he didn't like me because I was a Negro, I wouldn't have to bow down and feel inferior, it would just be a question of whether or not we could produce music together, which would be all I needed from him, and all he needed from me. Just to do that, and this is all that would be concerned. I had this problem with Scott LaFaro. He felt superior not only to Negroes but to whites as well.

"Charlie Haden was probably the most natural of all three white bass players I've ever used. The only thing that got Charlie confused was that he finally became aware that he was playing with Negroes and that made him paranoid, as if the situation were reversed, you know. He hadn't had enough experience as a man to know the difference between his talent and his origin.

"David Izenzon has a lot of background. I mean, he knows that he's Jewish, he knows his conception of that in relation to the human struggle. He has a feeling of superiority about his playing, playing with all those symphony orchestras, but he backed up that feeling of superiority with an ability to do anything that's possible to be done on the bass. Now that doesn't make him necessarily secure when he hears a person playing a very beautiful bass line that has more to do with hearing music than understanding it from a technical point of view. And hearing music is not the same thing as having the ability to do something that someone wants you to do, because you've first got to see what the person wants you to do before you do it. But to naturally just hear music because it's coming to you, no one is superior in that sense, regardless of who they are. I haven't found a black bass player that has the history of the instrument down like a lot of white people I've met, as far as the expression of it is concerned. Undoubtedly the string instruments have been one of the first expressions of a non-Negro world, because I find that almost all classical music is basically string music with the other instruments being used to elaborate on the strings. So that's got some sort of fact to it, about the difference between strings being a more expressive instrument to non-Negro, non-black people, than to black people mastering string instruments. I mean black people started playing Western instruments about the same time that, like, the saxophone and some other instruments were invented. Not like strings. Negroes, black people, haven't taken the string instrument as a part of their high ethnic expression. To them an instrument is an instrument and whatever you can express is what's happening. That's why I'm saying that I have to use mostly white bass players; I have never run into a black bass player that could keep up with my own growth in music. I haven't found a white bass player that could really keep up with that growth either, but what they could do is take the instruction, a very involved instruction, much faster and apply a certain line with what I'm doing simply because of knowing where to choose, what range of the instrument that they could use to play the music. That's the main thing with bass players.

"I think black people in America have a superior sense when it comes to expressing their own convictions through music. Most whites tend to think that it's below their dignity to just show suffering and just show any other meaning that has to do with feeling and not with technique or analysis or whatever you call it. And this to me is why the black man has developed in the field of music that the white man calls jazz. And basically I think that word, the sense of that word, is used to describe music that the white man feels is really inferior.

"But if you analyze the music itself, just from music for music, from notes for notes, it is a superior music as far as individual expression is concerned, jazz is. It's not a written music where you can show someone how, well, you just punch the button, or it's not a written music where the composer is dominating, and anyone can change what the composer is saying for betterment of themselves. It's only a label for them to let you know they are aware of either one of two things; they're trying to make you feel that they're giving you some sort of respect, to let you know that there's music that has come out of your race, or that there's a certain kind of music that you play that isn't like anyone else, and it's jazz. If people weren't what they were, they wouldn't have to use labels.

"But back to the bass player. What I have always wanted my bands to do is to have every man try to express *anything*, but yet at the same time show the thing that is allowing us to make music together, which has something to do with the person seeing in his mind the difference between making music total together or trying to make someone sound good, that's two different things. I don't like to do something just to make someone sound good because it's giving a false image of you. I like to let the total thing make the music, you know. As long as the guy is playing with me, I don't care how he does it. As long as they don't do anything to make me sound good but they get with the music, then that's beautiful. If they know a certain set way that they can play that will let the people know that they're with you, and you change your direction, then where are they going to be then? But when you change the direction and a person can go with you, that means he's getting more with the music than with you, more than with trying to make you sound good. With written music, the fact that it's written down makes everybody sound good because you just do what the guy told you, but with playing jazz it is different. Mostly, all rhythm instrumentalists have the idea that that's what they're supposed to do, play for the horn, and not to play music, you know. It's always been, 'Like, man, you didn't play that A7 down in the seventh bar.' 'Well, I was fucked up, I didn't know what to do,' right? But an instrument is an instrument and you've got to blend your instrument with other instruments to make music, not to give support to some other instrument simply because it needs your support to sound good.

"This doesn't really explain why I've had mostly white bass players, but it has something to do with it. I think it's got something to do with the fact that I've met more white bass players who could be free on their instrument than black bass players. Jimmy Garrison* is an example of this. One night we were playing at the Five Spot and he got fairly emotionally upset, cussed us out and said there wasn't a fucking thing happening with the music, you know, we were all full of shit and everything and for us all to stop and let him start playing. You know, like we're playing our ass off and the Five Spot is packed and he says, 'Stop this goddam music, ain't a fucking thing happening, what do you Negroes think you're doing? You going crazy, I mean it's nothing, you know, nothing's happening, what are you doing? I mean let me have it, I know what's happening.' All this, right in the middle of the Five Spot. And so we all stopped and he didn't play a note, so we all picked it back up from where he broke

* Garrison is the only Negro bassist Coleman has employed since he has been in New York.

in, you know. Now this doesn't have anything to do directly with being black or white; it has to do with a person's inferior feeling of what he thinks he's been left out of. Like, 'I know I can play the bass and yet you guys are doing something I don't know how to fit what I'm doing with.'

"It became a put-down. It's like the difference between what people call soul and what some other people call feeling. 'Cause everybody feels. You know, even an animal feels; you hit him hard and he'll respond. But soul is another thing. And people get feeling all mixed up with soul, because undoubtedly soul must have something to do with being very natural and feeling must have something to do with the choice of whether it hurt or didn't hurt or whether it made you happy or didn't make you happy. Choice that you can change. Soul must have something to do with where it's always positive and it's always complete. It doesn't need any elaboration on it. It happens twenty-four hours a day, and it's like a miracle. So with Jimmy, he's very soulful in the sense of his own conviction. Even when he said, 'Stop this fucking music, ain't nothing happening,' that meant right then and there that there was something happening with him that had a stronger meaning than what we were doing and he wanted to get with that. Which I thought was crazy, I mean, you know, I said, 'Well this cat is hip when we're cooking, and to him we ain't cooking now.'

"So when Jimmy called me up a couple of weeks later and said, 'Well, Ornette, Coltrane called me up with this gig and I want to take it with him,' I said, 'Well, go ahead, Jimmy. If you see a chance to better yourself, to make more money playing something you feel is right, then go ahead, because that's what it's all about.' "

When Ornette finally came out of retirement to play at the Village Vanguard in 1965, he played two new instruments publicly for the first time. He had learned to play trumpet and violin while in the woodshed, and sounded amazingly like himself on both instruments. He had learned to play the trumpet because his two protégés on that instrument were no longer available: Bobby Bradford had retired from music to go back to Texas to teach school, and Don Cherry was by then comfortably employed in Europe. The only other trumpet player Ornette had worked with since reaching musical maturity was Freddy Hubbard, who had played one of the two trumpet parts in the freely improvised double-quartet piece *Free Jazz*. Ornette surveyed the field and found no one playing trumpet whose approach to music was similar enough to his own to be useful. He would not hire one of the many glib, hard-bop-oriented trumpet players who were available, nor would he look for a younger trumpet player to train.

At the Vanguard, his sound on trumpet was curiously like Don Cherry's, who the critics had for years accused of sounding like Ornette Coleman: "One of the things that I have found out is that I could never get a trumpet player to play the exact range that I was writing for. Like, the trumpet is a physical instrument. Don is good and he can go high, he can play very high, but he wasn't what you'd call a first-trumpet player to take the high notes in a big band. Even among the first-trumpet players, I don't know anybody who can meet the physical requirements of being up every night. The trumpet players I have had haven't had the stamina and all that to meet all those requirements. What they have been is beautiful players. You don't have to be able to hit ten thousand high notes every night to be a beautiful player, you know. So I've always overlooked that. So that after Bobby and Don, I didn't see anybody who was, like, the same kind of beautiful players that they were, and nobody who could meet all the physical requirements either. So I just gave up on the trumpet."

Ornette also picked up on the violin, teaching himself from a book. Again, his violin lines came out sounding just like his saxophone lines, and were subjected to the same criticism that he had received in his early days of saxophone playing, specifically, that he couldn't play the instrument. But Ornette was not interested in playing Bach partitas; he was interested in playing Ornette Coleman. It was important to him to be able to play violin and trumpet so that he could be free to go in whatever musical direction he chose in the future. The string quartet had been an exasperating affair, because he had not been able to impart to four classically trained musicians just what the work was to achieve, the feeling, "the expression," which Ornette values more than all else in music. They had notes and they went from that; and when Ornette thought that they were going in the wrong direction, he was unable to correct them. He would play a figure for them on the alto saxophone, but that would not necessarily refer to the string instrument. He feels that he can now compose with a more intimate knowledge of the violin and that, in future compositions, he will be in a position to make demands on the musicians which he can illustrate.

The Village Vanguard engagement evoked accolades both from those friendly critics who thought that Ornette had done himself and the jazz industry a disservice by pricing himself out of the acceptable employment range, and from those conservatives who had finally, after five years of Ornette's presence in New York, come to regard him as an important musician. For Ornette, however, it was only a means to an end, that end being an escape from the American jazz scene. The job at the Vanguard did not meet Ornette's financial demands; his only intention in taking it had been to make enough money to leave the United States for an extended period of time.

At about the same time as the Vanguard engagement, Ornette had earned a five-figure sum for composing and producing the music for a film. His music was subsequently thrown out in favor of the classical Indian sitarist Ravi Shankar's, but he had acquired the money to make his getaway. In the late summer of 1965, Ornette left for Europe to see if he could make a better life for himself. In all probability, it will be the same experience as leaving Texas for Los Angeles, and Los Angeles for New York. The alienation will extend just one step further, the roots upended.

Ornette took Moffett and Izenzon with him, and he scheduled for the group a backbreaking tour of most of the major jazz festivals of Europe, all of which would take place within a two-week span. The first stop was England, and the situation there was familiarly ironic. He found himself the victim of an exchange clause in an agreement between the American and British musicians' unions. It seems that there is no union quota on the British-American exchange of musicians who qualify for work in symphony orchestras. Musicians employed for dances, however, must submit to a strict quota system based on an exact exchange between the two countries. It was this agreement between the unions that prohibited some British rock-'n-roll groups from entering the United States in 1965. Jazz, of course, qualifies as dance music under this agreement, even though there is no feasible way to work out a one-to-one exchange basis of jazz musicians under the system. Ornette was trapped in the quota. What followed was a situation in which he had to prove that he was *not* a jazz musician, or at least that he was a classical composer; he was required to write a work for woodwind quintet to qualify for the license to work in England.

After submission and approval of his work, Ornette was given a concert sponsored by a jazz and poetry group called New Departures, directed by the British poet Mike Horovitz. The concert was held at Croydon Hall in Fairfield, the large new modern collection of theater and concert halls just outside of London. Ornette was then further restricted by the musicians he could hire. Most of the "dance" musicians were prohibited from playing with him under the same license laws. Finally the work was performed; it was an artistic success but a financial failure.

The same could be said of Ornette Coleman's entire career as a jazz musician. It has been one long attempt to carve a place for his own particular self wherein he might work as himself with other individuals equally committed to themselves and to jazz as a whole: "If I was rich I wouldn't have to think that I'm fighting the system or that I was being exploited, because I could go out and do my best and be happy. If I was loved and felt that the people that gave me employment did so because they really wanted to see me do my best, I wouldn't have that problem either. But since I'm not loved and I'm not rich, I just feel fucked up, that's all. But being rich wouldn't make me play the saxophone any better, and I'm not loved because nobody is interested in what I'm doing; they're only interested in writing and talking about it, not the music itself.

"There is no music that can be performed unless somebody plays it. Whatever music you like or whether you like it or dislike it, somebody's got to perform it, and the performer is the man on the cross. There is no true place for the performer where his value and the value of the scene—the audience and the owners and the critics—is the same. It's always his need against the system, you know.

"And yet, if there was no performer, there would be no system in the business of music, right? But yet the performers don't see that. Well, for myself, I'm a Negro and I'm a jazz man. Performer or composer are secondary. And as a Negro and a jazz man, I just feel miserable.

"It's just that in vying for profit and making the price, everything has to be included, including the toilet paper. You can't get it free and you've got to use it. I know that money's not the solution, but if I could make money with what I'm doing, then that's even better for them because they could feel less guilty about it. They can say, 'Well, the bastard, at least they can't say we're stopping him from making money.'

"And I tell you, I would advise anybody that was sitting on their ass waiting for some wealthy middleman to come along and exploit them because they have talent, I would advise them to go out and do what they can do for themselves, and then they would know why that man is knocking on their door. Go out and see what you can do for yourself. If you've got to do something and you feel that it's just a matter of being tired of waiting for someone to come along and give you the chance to do it, don't wait for that. Go out and do it for yourself. Then you'll know."

III. HERBIE NICHOLS

THERE IS A KIND of culpability in the discovery of dead artists in that it seems almost criminal, certainly exploitative, even within the approved limits of capitalism, that the benefits of a man's work accrue to those who ignored him during his life. Certainly the Van Goghs, the Cézannes, and the Gorkys, after their deaths, hold no debts to those critics who fattened their reputations on their posthumous discoveries or to the merchants who fattened their wallets on after-the-fact accreditation. If an artist, in reproducing his own images, is able to instill them with enough life to be vital outside of his time, then a special value is created at his death because these life-images can never be created again. In this tradition, the artist must find satisfaction in his arti-fact, even if he receives neither remuneration nor recogni-tion during his lifetime.

The painter or poet has the advantage over the classical composer in that his work is physically the reproduction of itself, and therefore as permanent as any physical property:

Once written or painted, it will exist despite both the artist and his audience. But even classical composers who have complained about never hearing their work performed have a system of notation that assures them that their work will exist in the abstract even after their death. Mozart's reputation during his lifetime as an obscure composer for minor social functions did not prevent the survival of his work. Webern's work became an important influence on composers born many years after his death even though he himself never heard most of it performed.

The jazz musician has a different and more serious predicament. His work is the cultivation of the accidental. He cannot leave his work on paper, and any permanence he aspires to can take place only through the recording of his performance. He is both actor and playwright, composer, conductor, and featured soloist. If he is not employed, or if he is employed only under poor circumstances, then he does not create; and if he never has the security of a steady group that stays together at least long enough to learn his book (he composes for the men as much as for the horn, and they learn from the wild implementation of his book by improvising from it before a sympathetic audience), then his musical sensitivity and sensibility cannot evolve. The route of his work is through immediate communication with his audience; no paper, canvas, or written score is there to serve as intermediate agent.

Again we must point to the history of jazz as a workingman's music, in that the job itself is the opportunity for its expression. A month as the house pianist in a whorehouse, a band's tour of all the beer joints in the backwoods of Alabama, or two weeks' work in a New York bar cannot be approached in the same way as even the most modest concert hall, even if the results have equal value. The job is not where the jazz artist goes to earn the means of exploring his craft further; it is the place where his craft is applied; and that was the destruction of pianist and composer Herbie Nichols. For if the products of an artist's life work are to be the sum of his life, then Herbie Nichols, a jazz musician who seldom worked where he could play his own music and who has no records in the current catalogue, may be said not to have lived at all.

Herbie Nichols never had a year in his life when he came anywhere near supporting himself by playing either his own lyric and personal, but highly modern, jazz, or any of the sterile forms that club owners and bandleaders required him to play. In his last years, the most regular job that Herbie had in New York was at the Riviera, at that time a kind of clean hole in the sidewalk on Seventh Avenue in Greenwich Village, which featured a revivalist Dixieland band led by an obscure and inept drummer named Al Bandini. The Riviera, which no longer has a live-music policy, was known in the Fifties as a place where competent amateurs could sit in. It was then a hangout for Ivy League types, and on weekends, when they were out of school, they would come in with their trombones, clarinets, and crew-neck sweaters, surround Herbie, and call "When the Saints Go Marching In." There were times when such old-time swing musicians as banjoist Danny Barker or clarinetist Eddie Barefield would come by, perhaps with a singer; then the band might switch from Dixie to a lively spirited swing style. Herbie remembered: "There was life on those nights, but they were mostly dead nights." And this was the man whose piano playing and composing were as advanced as those of any musician working during the Forties and up until the late Fifties.

Actually, most of Herbie's jobs were even worse. The only others he held in New York in the year that he died, 1963, were backing a good singer named Sheilah Jordan at a lesbian bar on Seventh Avenue in the Village, and playing at a Harlem dive with Hal "Cornbread" Singer, one of the better postwar rhythm-and-blues tenor saxophonists. Singer was one of Herbie's staples, one of the few men who remembered him when they had jobs and needed an accomplished and reliable pianist. Herbie first worked with Singer in May 1943 at the Cafe Verona in Brooklyn. "This was before his 'Cornbread' days when he used to emulate Don Byas," Herbie said. It must have been this remembrance of a time when neither man had to change his style for reason of sustenance that kept them working together, if only intermittently.

Herbie was born in 1919 at 61st Street and 11th Avenue in Manhattan, in the area known as San Juan Hill. In the 1870's and 1880's, Negroes had settled where the ground begins to rise north of 51st Street, and the area had become a large black ghetto. Many of Teddy Roosevelt's Rough Riders were Negroes, and as there were constant fights between the blacks and the incoming Irish, they named the area San Juan Hill. Despite the Irish influx, the area remained black until the Harlem boom in the 1920's, when the Irish pushed the blacks north of 125th Street.

Herbie then moved, at the age of seven, to Harlem; and in his first year there he began his music instruction with a piano teacher named Charles L. Beck. The lessons continued for seven years. Beck was trained in classical music and wanted to push Herbie in that direction. Herbie's father had the same ambition for him. "During those early years," Herbie said, "I never attempted to play jazz. It was strictly *verboten* by the professor and my pa." He was a bright and eager kid and used to spend most of his time in the public library. The other kids on the block knew him as a marble shark, and he won a medallion one summer in a checker tournament (he lost it the day after). In high school, Herbie and some of his fellow students formed a small combo that, for a high school band, was regarded by the professionals as excellent.

In 1937, he joined the bassist George Duvivier in the famous Royal Baron orchestra. This seems to have been his first professional job. It was a young band that included, besides Duvivier, Nichols, and the leader Freddie Williams, altoist Elwyn Frasier, trumpeter George Tait, tenorman Mike Hedley, trombonist George Parker, baritone saxist Alton McDow, and drummer Rip Harewood. Herbie used to write some of the arrangements—they were so difficult that even he didn't want to sight-read them—but the band's primary arranger was Billy Moore, Jr., who wrote for the Royal Baron orchestra until he left to join Jimmy Lunceford's band. The Royal Baron was an advanced group, and it showed a lot of promise; but most of its members never reached their promised potential.

A more significant job was in 1938 at Monroe's Uptown House with alto saxophonist Floyd "Horsecollar" Williams, an old rhythm-and-blues player who was popular at the time. The advantage of working at Monroe's was that it was one of the centers of activity for the great musical reappraisal that was to culminate in the movement known as bebop, and Herbie Nichols was only one of many musicians who had joined the camp of young modernists who frequented Monroe's and Minton's. Lester Young, Kenny Kersey, and Dizzy Gillespie were among these revolutionists who jammed in

Monroe's while Herbie was there. Herbie wrote:* "The President [Lester Young] never coasted in those days. He was an eager beaver. Kenny Kersey used to play an extremely fast and modern octave style at the keyboard. At the time my head was chock full of 'classical vonce' and I, too, was fast and wild as lightning at the piano in my fascination of the competition around me."

But, and this was one of Herbie's main complaints, there were then as now cliques in jazz that determined who would work with whom. In the competition for jobs, it was difficult for sidemen to find work without belonging to one clique or another, and Herbie was not yet a leader. Speaking of belonging, Herbie said: "It seems like you either have to be an Uncle Tom or a drug addict to make it in jazz, and I'm not either one. Too many people allow themselves this affectation, play a role; that's no good."

Leonard Feather has reported that in the after-hours sessions Herbie was always being "pushed off the piano stool" by hipsters who were not his equal. For the three years after his tenure at Monroe's, he shopped around for work without much success.

In September of 1941 the draft caught Herbie, as it did many of the jazzmen of his generation, and he went overseas with the 24th Infantry Regiment. There was no leisure for practice in the army and, as he was not initially placed in a Special Services division, there were no musicians for him to play with. At this point, he thought of writing poetry, and he subsequently finished over fifty poems, most of them about unrequited love. He also did a great deal of reading; he calls himself, in his written sketch, "a poetaster and great

* Many of the direct quotations that appear here are from an autobiographical sketch Nichols once prepared in the hope that it would be needed for publicity purposes.

lover of all things scholarly." It was here that he began writing songs, and when he died he had over one hundred of
them on paper. "I've written calypso, waltz, blues, all kinds
of songs. In Africa whole villages sing; that's how it should
be. The voice is the most beautiful instrument of all; that's
why I'll always write songs." He later joined an army band
which included trumpeter Nelson Williams and some other
jazz musicians, and that made his tour a little easier.

Herbie felt enough love for America during his years
in the army to write some patriotic songs. He had felt the influence of the NAACP's "war on two fronts." This was a
campaign in which the loyalty and bravery of the Negro
soldier and the home-front efforts of respectable civic improvement groups like the NAACP would combine to create
for Negro Americans a less hostile country. These hopes, of
course, did not materialize, and returning soldiers found
America as hard on the black man as it ever had been. It was
after Herbie left the army in August of 1943 and returned to
look for work in New York that the disillusionment began
to set in.

The jobs that he worked on then were neither better
nor more frequent than those he had before he went into
the army. He went to work with a combo led by an alto saxophonist named Walter Dennis at Murrain's Cabaret in
Harlem. The group accompanied the singers and chorus line
of the regular stage shows, and played for dancing. Some
musicians did come by between the sets, but they were
mostly old-timers. Arranger Chappie Willets was one, and
the pianist Ellis Larkin another. It was during this period
that Herbie learned to play in more than one style. His interest was in bebop, but the only work he could find was
playing the older jazz.

He continued to see his old friend Billy Moore, Jr., from

the Royal Baron band. Moore had by now established himself as an arranger, and had written some of Lunceford's
most successful tunes: "Belgium Stomp," "What's Your Story
Morning Glory," "Chopin's Prelude No. 7," "Buggs Parade,"
and "Monotony in 4 Flats." Having left Lunceford, he had
done some arranging for Charlie Barnett's orchestra. He was,
in fact, in great demand; bandleaders such as Jan Savitt and
Tommy Dorsey were always calling him. Even so, there was
little he could do for Herbie.

In mid-1944, Herbie left Murrain's and went to work at
Ernie's Three Ring Circus in Greenwich Village. That job
lasted from September to December. Herbie noted: "They
were horrible jobs. There were good musicians on some of
them, but we couldn't play any music, not even any decent
swing-style music. The music was only supposed to get the
job done, keep time for the girls, back up the singers, keep
the people dancing; and there was so much happening. I
mean Parker and Monk and those people were really changing things. I kept hoping that things would get better, that
I would have more opportunities, but they just never seemed
to come."

On another occasion, he said: "Critics didn't help
either. I don't mean this only for myself, but look what a hard
time bop had getting through. People who were making it
off swing, people like Benny Goodman, were able to hold it
back. It was years before the bop records got through. The
critics could have helped a lot if they hadn't been so much
against it."

The next job was more like it. Bobby Booker had a
combo at the Elks' Rendezvous in Harlem that was more
bebop-oriented and included the excellent baritone-alto
saxophonist Sahib Shihab. It was a six-month job in which
Herbie played music that was close to his own. But next

came the beginning of what was to be a long list of road engagements, this time in Philadelphia, to work at the Midway Musical Bar with trumpet player Herman Autry, who was best known for his work with Fats Waller.

There was a reason for Herbie's growing popularity with the older-style musicians: "The swing musicians and even the New Orleans musicians had resisted bebop, sure, but they did prefer to use the more modern drummers if they could adapt to the old style. That meant the bass and piano had to know both styles too."

In 1945 and 1946 it looked as if Herbie's career might be opening up. Herbie Nichols was finally recorded. His first date was with Danny Barker for Apollo records. He also worked in Brooklyn with Hal Singer, but from that modern scene Herbie's engagement at the Village Vanguard sent him back in time again; his leader was Freddie Moore, a drummer who had played in New Orleans with King Oliver.

In December of 1946 it was the dance circuit with Illinois Jacquet in Detroit, Philadelphia, and at the Howard Theatre in Washington, D.C. That was essentially a swing band with some bebop influence. Jacquet was a great crowd-pleaser who was immensely popular during the Forties, when his tenor saxophone duels with Flip Phillips had crowds tearing up the theaters during "Jazz at the Philharmonic" tours. Jacquet was out of Basie, only he was an even harder swinger than most of Basie's sidemen. The band that Illinois took with him then was a strong one, about evenly balanced between bebop and swing. Shadow Wilson, the drummer, went both ways. Trombonist J. J. Johnson and baritone saxophonist Leo Parker had been in the first wave of the bebop revolution. Bassist Al Lucas was more conservative, and Russell Jacquet, Illinois' brother, sang and played trumpet. All that Herbie said about that tour was, "It wasn't miserable."

Herbie had been writing and working on his style all through this period: "I thought then that I was ready, and I looked around to find some work as a leader. I wanted to get my thing across. But somehow things never seemed to fall my way. The owners used to think that I was too far out. I've actually had guys tell me that they would hire me if I changed my style. Now I didn't mind playing any style when I was working for somebody else. I think it's good for a musician to be able to play more than one way—it gives you more things you can do in your own style. But if it's going to be the Herbie Nichols Trio, then it's going to be Herbie Nichols' music."

He knew Thelonious Monk; during this time they talked a lot and listened to one another's work. Monk was then one of the saints of bebop, a composer and teacher to whom most of the young musicians looked for fresh ideas. Herbie saw Monk's music for what it was: a serious advancement in jazz, and a great individual expression. He thought that there was room for development, however: "Monk is a good example of how irresponsible critics are. Now I like Monk. He's a friend of mine and a great composer and musician. I wrote Monk up for a Negro magazine, the *Music Dial*, back in 1946 before he had recorded for Blue Note. I was honest. I knew people hadn't caught on to him, but I raved about him anyway. Leonard Feather and those other people didn't even know what he was doing; they hated him. Nowadays if you say anything against Monk you're a dog. But do you know that Monk's music hasn't changed from 1939 until now? That shows critics haven't been doing what they're responsible to do."

In 1947 markets were starting to close up for Herbie

just as they were opening for the rest of the beboppers. Herbie said, "I free-lanced locally the whole year and took things just a bit easier than I had in the past," meaning that he could find no work. He did meet bandleader John Kirby in December, and played with his group at the Royal Roost in New York. In 1948 he worked with Johnny Felton, whom he described as "a hustling, blues-loving drummer." Aaron Bell was with the group for a while, and Herbie thought Aaron was "a bassist who is a thorough musician with a fine all-around intelligence." Herbie was teaching piano for money now, and he did get to lead his own group at a few dances in New York that year.

In 1949 it was back on the road, with more conservative musicians. First stop was the Continental in Milwaukee with a band led by the affluent John Kirby. Buster Bailey, Nelson Williams, and Walter Bishop (the drummer, not the pianist) were also in the group. In July he was accompanying Maxine Sullivan with Snub Mosley (known as the Man with the Funny Horn, for a tune he played on slide saxophone) in Morgantown, West Virginia, at the Chest Lake Supper Club. The next job was in late November in Rock Island, Illinois, where Herbie rejoined John Kirby in a quartet. They toured Wisconsin and Illinois, playing Decatur, Sheboygan, Racine, Milwaukee, and other towns.

In 1950 there was no work playing what was by then being called progressive jazz. Herbie did make two records, one with trumpeter Bobby Mitchell (with whom he also had some club work) for Mercury Records, and some straight rhythm-and-blues recordings with saxophonist Charlie Singleton and trumpet player Frank Humphreys, for Decca and Abbey records respectively. In December he went to Boston for the first time, where he played the Hi-Hat with Snub Mosley.

Back in New York in 1951, Herbie went out again to the nightclubs and record companies with his charts. There were no takers. For some reason Herbie was never able to understand, he could interest no one in his music, either in midtown, where the bebop clubs, led by Birdland, were flourishing, or in Harlem, where there were still jobs for the lesser-priced modern musician. He was in demand as a sideman only among the conservatives who respected his high musicianship, reading ability, and adaptability.

Edgar Sampson, who had played alto saxophone and violin with Duke Ellington, Fletcher Henderson, and Chick Webb, and who was best known for composing some of the most successful instrumentals of the Thirties ("Blue Lou," "Stomping at the Savoy" and "Lullaby in Rhythm"), called him for work at the Club 845 in the Bronx. The club had gained some national notoriety through a hard-blowing record called "The 845 Stomp." Edgar Sampson played swing arrangements and, while Herbie was with him, expanded his swing book to accommodate the mambo rage which New York was experiencing as a result of the mass immigration of Puerto Ricans and Cubans. Sampson had done arrangements for Tito Rodriguez and Tito Puente. Herbie had no trouble mastering the mambo and even found it stimulating, for it brought him a new appreciation of the possibilities of one of his favorite instruments, the drum. He adapted the mambo to his own idiom, wrote five mambos, and decided to experiment with other Latin rhythms using modern-jazz material. One such tune was "Debra's Tango," of which he was very proud, but which he never got to record.

There were jobs in 1951 with Lucky Thompson, undoubtedly the most significant reed player Herbie ever worked with. Herbie also tried some straight commercial work in that year: he had seen Edgar Sampson make a reasonable income by writing for various acts. He said, "Following Sampson's example, I broke out my score pad and penned a few arrangements for various vaudeville acts, mainly ventriloquist Sammy Hines and dancer Foster Johnson." But this too led to a dead end.

The next year, Thelonious Monk introduced Herbie to Mary Lou Williams, whose piano and compositional work was, in 1952, quite avant-garde. Mary Lou was recording often and was being booked regularly in first-rate jazz clubs. She was getting concerts all over the country, and her style, though eclectic, was unusually broad and deep. Later she was to experience the capriciousness of the jazz industry, and by the late Fifties people were asking, "What ever happened to Mary Lou Williams?" But in 1952, the novelty of a woman jazz musician who was not a singer and who was actually extending the forms of jazz made her a good item for entrepreneurs and for the jazz press.

It was this breadth that attracted her to Herbie Nichols' music. He played from his book for her, and, impressed by the musically fresh, sound ideas that Herbie showed her, she recorded some of his tunes. One, "The Bebop Waltz" (which she retitled "Mary's Waltz"), was one of the first waltz-time tunes in the modern idiom. She also used "Stennell," which she retitled "Opus 2" (both Atlantic releases). On the Circle label she recorded "At Da Function." These records gave Herbie, at 33, a modest reputation as a composer of unusual talent whose compositions had never been used.

Herbie got work in Cleveland, leading a trio at such clubs as Jack's Bar and the Club Tiajuana. Returning to New York, he made his first record date as a leader with a quartet that included drummer Shadow Wilson. It was a 78 rpm, "S'Wonderful" on one side, and a composition of Herbie's

own entitled "Whose Blues" on the other. "It was an im-
promptu deal cooked up at the studio with no rehearsals
whatsoever," he wrote later. The reception in *Down Beat*
was lukewarm—it was given three stars in the magazine's
possible-five-star rating system. But this opening to the future closed almost immediately; the only work he could find
that year was with the same conservatives who had hired
him most regularly before. His friend Danny Barker, the
banjoist, brought him into Jimmy Ryan's, a New York Dixieland house, to fill out a group that included such old-line
musicians as Arthur Herbert, clarinetist Eddie Barefield,
trumpeter Doc Cheatam, and trombonist George Stevenson.
Then, trombonist Milton Larkin called him to tour Washington, D.C., and some places in the backwoods of Maryland,
which might best be described as raunchy. That was straight
gutbucket music: "We played nothing but the blues. I took a
lot of kidding about playing such authentic blues and claim-
ing New York as my birthplace." In the summer, it was with
Esmond Samuels, playing what Herbie called "nontax-
ing" music in Hagerstown, Maryland, and Chester, Pennsylvania. He went from there to Buffalo for a few weeks with
a trio that he described as strange. At the end of 1952, it
was Boston's Savoy in a nondescript quartet headed by a
trumpeter named Joe Thomas, and including Anderson
Chambers on trombone, Art Trappier on drums, and clarinetist Pete Clark, a group with which Herbie recorded for
Atlantic records.

There was little variation in Herbie's career between
1952 and 1955. He worked exclusively on the East Coast, and
only once with modern musicians—in Philadelphia at the
Showboat with Sonny Stitt. He wrote and accompanied
some dance arrangements at the Latin Casino in Philadelphia, and then he went back to Boston with Rex Stewart and

Alvin Nichols. The very proficient tenor saxophone honker Arnett Cobb took Herbie to southern Maryland, Washington, D.C., and Montreal. Then it was Philadelphia, Baltimore, and Bethlehem, Pennsylvania, providing filler for the big open tone of tenor saxophonist Big Nick Nicholas.

By spring 1954 Herbie had retrogressed completely in terms of the quality and importance of the musicians he worked with. He found himself at the Savoy in Boston again, this time with Wilbur de Paris' New Orleans jazz band. He worked seven cold weeks there, and returned to New York with that band for twenty-two weeks at Jimmy Ryan's. It was revivalist Dixie at its most frigid and commercial. I once asked Herbie if the music interested him, and he replied with a succinct "No." He said, "I had to work that out of me by playing grease with Horsecollar Williams." They worked the Safari, a neighborhood club in Harlem. Herbie remembers Juanita Hall coming by to hear ". . . the uninhibited 'Horse' wail 'far out' blues. Also to hear my rendition of Avery Parrish's 'After Hours.' "

From there it was back to Dixie and Boston with Conrad Janis and his Tailgaters. One might think that by then Herbie would have given up all ambitions of playing new jazz. After all, the bebop spirit had died, or had been appropriated first by "cool," or progressive, jazz, and then by the developing hard-bop school of East Coast jazz. Herbie was now an anachronism, a man whose age for development would seem to have been bypassed during the Forties, when bebop was in its bud. The leading pianists of that generation—John Lewis, Bud Powell, and Thelonious Monk (also a legend then, but at least a recorded one)—seemed to have resolved all the problems of keyboard bebop improvisation, and had already influenced a younger generation of pianists. This was true especially of Lewis and Powell.

Herbie had never stopped studying, though, and had been keeping his ear open to new forms of music all the time. He had listened to Stravinsky, Copland, and Milhaud (though there is little apparent influence by any of the three on his music), and he had been studying African music, which he considered the key to jazz.

He also had been auditioning for clubs and for record companies. "I begged Al Lion ten years for a record, but I was 36 before I ever recorded. He said I was the most persistent man he ever met. But he's one of the most open-minded of them all." Lion, co-owner of Blue Note, contracted the best rhythm men in the business: Art Blakey, Al Mc-Gibbin, Teddy Kotick, and Max Roach. Herbie recorded 25 of his compositions in four sessions between May and August, 1956, and the result was two sets of what must be some of the finest piano trio music in recorded jazz.

The reviews were better than favorable. Martin Williams wrote in *Down Beat:* "He has dealt so well with so many problems often neglected by other jazz musicians. He is original . . . it is obvious he plays with a jazz style that is thoroughly his own. The things he can do with time and the fact that his rhythm and harmonies are interrelated, indeed inseparable, are exceptional. He is not at all interested in currently 'hip' tempos, mannerisms, or finger dexterity, and he shows that he is not at all afraid of a steady 'four' rhythm, of a modernized version of a simple Thirties 'riff time' conception, of a swing bass—and that he can bring such things off.

"As a composer he may work . . . with basically simple and brief ideas. He has the capacity to turn and phrase them off with originality, and he can develop them compositionally. He can do the same in improvising."

Larry Gushee said later in the *Jazz Review* that Herbie

Nichols was ". . . certainly an original stylist, he plays as if conversing with himself. That is to say, he'll play a short phrase of the tune, interpose an angular, rather dissonant motive, combine this with an elusive mumbling in his left hand. Herbie likes to build his tunes . . . around emotional situations that are attractively heartfelt and natural. . . . He has the advantage . . . [of] richness of experience and varied musical contrast. . . ."

The first set of two 10-inch lp's released by Blue Note had little financial success despite the favorable reviews: After nine years, Blue Note still has some of the first pressing. The same is true of the 12-inch lp, taken from the same sessions, which was released a year later. On its release Nat Hentoff congratulated Blue Note for issuing this third set despite the financial failure of the first two. These records established Herbie Nichols among the jazz cognoscenti, and those musicians with whom he had recorded spread his name among the general community of modern jazz musicians. Apart from Blakey, Roach, and the others present on the Blue Note dates, only a few musicians, notably Gigi Gryce and Charlie Mingus, had encouraged him to continue playing in his own style.

Herbie's style seems to fall, in a musicological sense, between those of Teddy Wilson and Thelonious Monk. He has the keyboard dexterity, the clarity, the sonorous tone, and the elegant, well-developed melodies of Wilson. The resemblance to Monk, his contemporary, is more apparent, though the equally apparent differences make it obvious that Monk was not Herbie's influence. The dissonances and a kind of melodic structure based on a preconceived rhythmic development which are common to both pianists were potent in the early Fifties, and Monk and Herbie were two of the very few to exploit that potency. Herbie also made an LP on the Bethlehem label with Danny Richmond, a drummer known for his work with Charlie Mingus. But Bethlehem is now defunct, and that record is almost impossible to obtain. Still, based solely on the Blue Note releases, one probably could get most critics and musicians to testify that Herbie Nichols was a major pianist and composer.

Listening to such tunes as "House Party Starting," "Lady Sings the Blues" (which Billie Holliday recorded), "Terpsichore," and the "Third World," I am convinced that if Herbie had been a more publicized musician, he would have been an important influence on that generation of pianists that came along in the Fifties, and possibly that he would have provided an alternative to the John Lewis and Bud Powell approaches which dominated the period.

"House Party Starting," with Max Roach and Al Mc-Kibbon, is an unusually sensitive track. It is a lovely, simple tune repeated over and over with very slight shading in tempo and color. By these subtle repetitions, Herbie focuses and refocuses the listener's attention on all the various implications of the one idea. It is an exclusive kind of improvisation, a structure of containment that manages a mirrored movement of emotional matter from a single thematic base. There is a relaxed quality to the rhythm accompaniment, but all the action is integrated into the melodic development. Herbie had a great appreciation for the function and heritage of the drum. He always talked of scoring for the drum, and in "House Party Starting" he did it so well that Max Roach was able to assume responsibilities that are not generally associated with drums. In "Terpsichore," for example, Roach actually finishes the melodic line at the end, like a horn.

These records led to one job playing modern music in 1956, in a now-defunct Greenwich Village nightclub. The appearance was reviewed in the *Intro Bulletin* by George H. Morse: "He does not belong to any group. Working out his complicated tonally and rhythmically reiterative style while blowing piano in all the . . . jazz grooves, he is never on the outside but in the distance. . . . Herbie Nichols always loses part of his audience, but the rest are sucked in, dizzified by the music."

That job seems to have been the end of Herbie's career as a modern jazz musician. As before, he was always hounding the record companies with an ever-growing portfolio of original compositions. But there is something commercially deadly about a record that excites the in crowd but makes no dent on the money-paying jazz audience.

From there it was Jimmy Ryan's again with the Dixie musicians. Bassist Buell Neidlinger says he met Herbie at Ryan's, but that by then Herbie was not discussing his own ideas of music even though that music still was foremost in his mind. Although he was showing his poems to those whom he trusted, he maintained a complete separation between the music he played and the music he cared about. Neidlinger said, "If he had played his own music, they would have run him out of those places."

The next and final time Herbie was to play modern music was at a Greenwich Village loft benefit in 1962, in a pick-up group that included Archie Shepp and bassist Ahmad Abdul Malik. I spoke to him at that session, and he was amazed that there were so many people present who knew and respected his music.

In 1962, Herbie made a tour of Scandinavia with a hodgepodge of Dixieland musicians who achieved an easy kind of success in concert halls, universities, and in a few bars. Occasionally he lectured on his own music and performed some trio selections, but for the most part he was an accompanist for the conservatives. He considered that tour one of the best things that ever happened to him, even though he brought back no money.

He said later that the next best thing that ever happened to him was the interview with him that I was preparing for *Metronome* magazine. This was 1963, in the early spring: "Do you know that I've never been written up? I read the magazines and I see write-ups on everybody. All kinds of guys have articles written on them, and I know that I must be better than some of those guys. I know some people who think I'm important, musically. Well I don't know about that, but they say I'm a nice guy but I don't carry myself right. Now what does that mean? Anyway, I've never been written up."

He was aware of a deep physical illness when I saw him, though the doctors had not yet settled on leukemia as the source. Herbie would be enthusiastic for a few minutes about his chances for finally breaking through, but then the sickness would enter his face and his voice would be occupied by the despair of being abused by the music industry for twenty-five years. It would deepen when he discussed the music he was so immensely proud of, and he would bring out manuscripts to show that he had been productive despite the lack of opportunity to show his work. He was likewise proud of his general musicianship, and he made severe demands on those musicians whom he respected, Thelonious Monk included. He thought no jazz musician, no matter how talented, could be considered a finished musician without a working knowledge of music notation: "I'd like to see jazz musicians start reading. It's a wide world, but I don't see where there's been that much musical progress. Ellington made a real contribution, just as Dizzy Gillespie and Parker did, but you study all that now and it's all really very simple, even some of the things Gillespie and Parker did, and there's nothing to Dixie. But so many jazz musicians, so many colored musicians that is, can't read. I have some friends who are tremendous composers by what they are able to hear, but they can't read. All they have is their musical heritage. So as far as composing goes, you can say they're not even musicians. That's where the white fellow has it over us. But some of our guys, like Billy Taylor, have the training but can't appreciate the proper function of the drums. I can't say it too much: That's where the future lies—in arranging a broader use of drums.

"Now John Lewis is a guy who has both the training and the feeling for jazz. He's got a Master's degree. I really respect that. I wish I had had the chance to get that kind of training. But with all his training John Lewis seems like he's forgotten how to use drums in his melody and harmony."

Herbie's prerequisite for the attainment of the summit in musicianship presents a paradox for both white and black musicians. "But for my own music, the white fellows have grasped what I'm doing right away, guys like Don Ellis and so many others. They get what I'm doing faster than the colored fellows." Yet, in application: "The white just don't have the heritage that the colored fellows have and the colored fellows don't have the training that the white guys have, and you can't play good jazz and compose good jazz without either. I don't know, though, there have been a lot of guys who were able to make what I call a natural contribution because they had a feeling. But so many haven't been accepted and have had to go on dope or go crazy or become almost subtle Uncle Toms to make it, and, what's worse, have lost contact with themselves."

It was this cognizance of self that Herbie valued most, and used to keep his music alive in all those years of wasted performances. He held tightly to his Afro-American background: "I think musicians ought to be more interested in African music. I know I learned from it. I listen to it for pleasure. The genius of African music makes me proud to be of African derivation. Our drummers ought to learn to use that genius and all jazz musicians ought to learn to use the drums more, especially the tympani. That's the most important part of our musical heritage. I like to compose for drums, to integrate the drum into the melody, that's how it is in African music. The drums have more to do than just be metronomes. Can you imagine playing with those gourds and rattles and palm leaf spines, like the Africans? If I was arranging for an orchestra I'd use that kind of rhythm, while the tune could be going some place else."

Herbie's concept of his cultural identification traced, in a sense, the course of the Middle Passage during slavery. He had written in the liner notes for the 12-inch set on Blue Note: "Having been born and raised in Manhattan almost gives me a feeling of being cognizant of a type of music that might even be called New York jazz. My parents came to these shores from St. Kitts and Trinidad and were part of the large influx of British subjects who settled in Gotham during the period of the first World War. The first songs that I ever heard were 'Sly Mongoose,' 'The West Indian Blues,' and similar other chants. In the subculture of this particular environment, my early diet and upbringing were quite special things. As a matter of fact I've written a couple of calypsos, entitled 'Crackup' and 'I Worship Delilah.' . . . Perhaps that is why I've always particularly enjoyed the exotic styles of Denzil Best and Thelonious Monk, in whose music I can trace this influence of my youthful years."

Herbie thought that all jazz musicians should conscientiously seek out and analyze the masters of the past. "One should be willing to enjoy and study all of the great jazz musicians of the past and present. In addition, each one of these artist's limitations should be pinpointed and analyzed."

The results of this study of African, West Indian, classical, and modern jazz would be the achievement of a quintessential quality that would make identity clear: "There are reasons why the best jazz must 'sound' the same as it did in the beginning. I keep remembering that the overtones of 'fifths' created by the beautiful tones of any ordinary tuned drum was purely the first music—the precursor of the historic major scale, no less, which was built on the same principles. That is why the cycle of 'fifths' is so prevalent in elemental jazz. In other words, in a great desire to 'sound,' the beginner at improvisation grasps at easy and fundamental aural pleasures.

"And so, after tracing this elementary history of 'sound,' we can readily understand why drummers start to 'drop bombs' to usher in the new music of Charlie Parker, Dizzy Gillespie, and Bud Powell. Each 'bomb' created a newly rich and wholly unexpected series of overtones, beginning in the lower registers. These rich syncopations were fitting accompaniments to the supplemental overtones played by the horns in the higher registers. That is why the pianists became so percussive with their left hands. Among modern drummers, Art Blakey is considered invaluable. He astounds me when it comes to being in tune. I can hear overtones from his snare drum, cymbals, rimshots, everything he touches. Sometimes he 'pounds' some of these recalcitrant instruments in tune when the atmosphere is unsteady. I've seen Denzil Best rub his bass drumhead with a damp cloth at the start of a gig. He spoke of a 'whoooosh' effect that he sought. This effect that he achieves, plus his musical discipline, makes him also one of the best tubmen around today. I'm sure that this is also one of the prime reasons for Sonny Greer's great value to the Ellington orchestra for so many years. The jazz sound is surely a living thing and as a piano player I find it mostly in old uprights. Sometimes these faded pianos with muted strings, strange woodwork, and uneven 'innards' have a way of giving up fast and resonant overtones. Each note shoots back at you like a bass drum. In such situations, as soon as I find that I am not financially liable, I let myself go and use any kind of unorthodox touch needed to dig out the strange 'sounds' which I know are in the instrument."

The Chinese axiom "Learn from the past and learn from abroad" describes Herbie's method of study. He wrote in *Metronome* magazine in February, 1956: "Think of what can be done with the sounds of the multiple counterpoint of Hindemith, the neo-classic polytonality of Shostakovitch and Piston and the melting of the vast musical devices which Bartók loves to use at random and which make his kaleidoscopic style come closest to jazz.

"But jazz has come a long way since 'the stomp.' A lot of myths have been dispelled and we find countless master jazzists who are masters of classical music as well. Time signatures are altered freely nowadays. For instance, I am beginning to learn that certain tunes that I write cannot become alive, even for one chorus, unless I score the drum part fittingly. Specific suspensions and inversions must be explicitly indicated or else I find that there is no 'sound.'"

Yet when I talked to Herbie, it was clear that he thought nothing could come of all this preparation unless the whole environment of jazz was changed. A large part of this is due to differences between the musicians themselves—differences between contemporaries, and between members of the various generations that are still active in the jazz industry. Herbie summed it up: "It seems that if everybody, especially the colored musicians, just by understanding their own problems, would seek each other out, they might work something out. But they don't, and that's really sad. When bop came out, Duke Ellington and Count Basie and those guys who were making it should have taken those guys to heart—made it easier for them. Now Duke was tremendous in using African music in his own band, but it seems like he wasn't conscious of the history of African music in these new fellows. Everybody's always shoving for himself instead of trying to help the other fellow out. That's why we never get anywhere."

Herbie never got anywhere, except to Blue Note records for one period in the spring and summer of 1955. When I saw him last, in his sister's apartment in a low-income district in the Bronx, he seemed to be dying of disillusionment. He knew his worth, but it seemed that nobody else did, at least nobody that could improve his condition. The last thing he said to me was: "I'm not making $60 a week. I'm trying to sell some copyrights, but if you don't have somebody behind you in this country, you die. I wish I could get some African government, Ghana, for instance, interested in my music and to give me a job teaching, maybe; now that would be a very good thing." It was typical of Herbie Nichols' life that *Metronome*, the magazine for which I was preparing the first article ever written on him, folded before the article could be published. By the time I placed it elsewhere, Herbie had died.

IV. JACKIE McLEAN

THE OTHER MUSICIANS treated in this book have all
been outsiders throughout their jazz careers. They have
never been involved with the mainstream of jazz playing,
and they have never been a part of the various coteries that
make up that mainstream. Herbie Nichols grew up in the
jazz center of the world, but was ignored by his contemporaries for reasons that are still not clear to me, except that
his music was not fashionable. The adversities and ironies
that have characterized Cecil Taylor's and Ornette Coleman's careers have been the predictable result of the conscious assimilation in their music of elements alien to the
mainstream. These men are all innovators, and innovation
breeds adversity. Taylor and Coleman, at least, never expected anything else; they knew early in their careers that
their music would offend a substantial part of the jazz establishment.

But Jackie McLean has never considered himself an
innovator, nor have the analysts of his time considered him

one. He is certainly an individualist, having one of the most distinctive tones and phraseologies on the modern alto saxophone, and his playing and composing have never been anything but contemporary. But although he has been a member of the various jazz vanguards of the last seventeen years, he has never been the man who provoked the abrupt upheavals that forced and formed the vanguard. Unlike Coleman and Taylor, who are often accused of being esoteric and arrogant, respectively, by many of their fellow musicians, and the relatively unknown Herbie Nichols, Jackie McLean has commanded the respect of jazz musicians, promoters, and followers since his late teens. He was raised in the hothouse of modern jazz, and before he turned twenty he could count among his friends and associates most of the big names of modern jazz. He went to high school with Sonny Rollins; at seventeen he was a student of the great Bud Powell; at eighteen he was a protégé of Charlie Parker; at nineteen he was tutoring Miles Davis on East Coast attire; before he was twenty-five he was thought by many musicians to be Charlie Parker's heir apparent on the alto saxophone.

Jackie McLean is said to have "paid his dues," meaning that he has worked his way up through the more respected bands, and that he has suffered all the slings and arrows of the jazz life. He has held jobs and recorded with Charlie Parker, Miles Davis, Bud Powell, Thelonious Monk, Charlie Mingus, Art Blakey, and many, many more top modern jazz musicians. As for his "heavy dues," Jackie was a drug addict for much of his adult life, yet he has managed to raise three children who are conspicuous among other teen-agers only for their sanity.

Jackie McLean at thirty-five is still a growing man. In the last few years, he has become a leader whose records sell consistently, and who would be in considerable demand for nightclub work were it not for the fact that he was handicapped by his situation as a jazz musician without a cabaret card, which is roughly analogous to being a fisherman without a boat. This restriction forbids him to work in nightclubs in New York City, the biggest jazz market in the world. Jackie expects to have his cabaret license by the time this book is released, and he will then be able to accept some of the offers which, until now, he has been obliged to decline.

The reason for Jackie McLean's presence in these pages is not only that he exemplifies much of the best and the worst of the jazz life but also that he is one of the few jazz musicians who has been able to keep his music fresh and moving for more than a decade and a half.

Jackie McLean was born John McLean, Jr., in New York City on May 17, 1931, the son of John McLean and Alpha Omega McLean. His father was a guitarist of some repute, having worked with such swing musicians as Tiny Bradshaw and saxophonist Teddy Hill. Hill was one of the pivotal bandleaders of the late Thirties, but he is probably better known for operating Minton's ("the birthplace of bebop"), a bar that was easily the most seminal establishment of the bebop revolution. By the time Jackie was eleven, the McLeans had lived on 135th Street, 111th Street, 114th Street and Seventh Avenue, and 117th Street.

Jackie has little recollection of his father; he says that he can remember seeing him only about three times in his life. According to his mother, John McLean used to lock himself in a room with Jackie, sit him up on the dresser, and play the guitar to him. One wintery day John slipped on the ice and hit his head on the curbstone; he died soon after in Harlem Hospital of a concussion. Jackie was seven at the time.

Mrs. McLean did what she could. She worked as a

domestic while pursuing her education until she qualified as a laboratory technician. She was later to become a school-teacher, and continues teaching today. When Jackie was twelve, she remarried, and took her only child to live with her new husband on 158th Street and St. Nicholas Avenue in the heart of Harlem's Sugar Hill, though the area was by then considerably less elegant than it had been some ten or fifteen years before, when it was the haven of successful black people. After Stitt Junior High, Jackie went on to Benjamin Franklin High School.

There never was a time when music was not in Jackie's life. His stepfather, Jimmy Briggs, owned a record shop at 141st Street and Eighth Avenue that specialized in jazz. The family attended the Abyssinian Baptist Church, the pulpit of which Adam Clayton Powell, Sr., had passed on to his son five years before. Jackie's godfather, Norman Cobbs, played saxophone in the church band, and when young Jackie begged Cobbs for use of one of his two saxophones, he was given the straight silver one, a soprano, much to his disap-pointment. Jackie's mother was at first opposed to the idea of his learning to play the horn, calling his father a "no-good musician." Briggs took a more positive stand and tried to develop some musical taste in the fifteen-year-old. Jackie had heard only those musicians who were broadly publi-cized, and considered Charlie Barnett, Illinois Jacquet, Charlie Ventura, and Flip Phillips the titans of saxophone playing. Briggs brought home recordings of the better swing musicians, and introduced Jackie to the likes of Lester Young, Johnny Hodges, Ben Webster, and Coleman Haw-kins. Jackie's early preference was for Lester Young, and he has never shaken that influence.

He was given an alto saxophone on his fifteenth birth-day, and has been with it ever since. In maturity, he was to pick up the soprano saxophone briefly, but in his teens he was unable to take it seriously as a musical instrument because it was neither golden nor curved. He studied at one of those unaccredited music schools for twenty-five cents a lesson under Walter "Foots" Thomas, Cecil Scott, and Joe Napoleon, and his playing at the time consisted of copying licks from tenor saxophonists Lester Young and Ben Webster. It seems that he had really wanted a tenor saxophone all along, as he disliked the sound he had heard in all the professional alto saxophonists. Jackie said: "The first thing I was involved with when I first got my alto saxophone was the sound, trying to make the alto not sound like an alto. I was trying to make it sound like a tenor because I really wanted a tenor before I heard Bird [Charlie Parker]. I would go to my room, and I had a little hat that I fixed like a porkpie like Prez's [Lester Young] hat. I used to put my hat on and look at myself in the mirror because I had some pictures of Prez that I used to cut out; I had a scrapbook at that time. Most kids collected pictures of ballplayers and things like that, I used to collect pictures of Prez. I guess he was like Ringo Starr of the Beatles to me. But the funny thing is, I never saw Lester Young until 1948, and I had seen Bird before that. I was too young to go anywhere at the time, and I can't remember him playing anywhere in New York. He was in the army in '46 when I first started going out. But trying to imitate Lester Young and Dexter Gordon on an alto saxophone is what got my sound to be the way it is."

Jackie's playing at this time consisted entirely of copying, and one of his favorites was Dexter Gordon's solo on "Blowing the Blues Away" with the Billy Eckstine band. Because he thought the tone of the pre-Charlie Parker alto saxophonists—such as Willie Smith, Johnny Hodges, and Tab

Smith—too light and syrupy, he was working most of all on his tone.

The year was 1946, and the principles of jazz improvisation were undergoing a vast overhauling from several different directions. It was now more than six years since Charlie Parker had first worked at the famous after-hours cabaret Monroe's Uptown House, and four years since he had played the Savoy Ballroom with the Jay McShann band. The Billy Eckstine band, which brought so many of the early bebop musicians together, was by the next year defunct, and Parker, Bud Powell, Thelonious Monk, Dizzy Gillespie, and many others had done considerable recording. Bebop had already been so-named, and Miles Davis was beginning to established a strong presence. Jazz clubs within walking distance of Jackie's house were abundant, even though McLean was far too young to be admitted to them. The new music was played at Minton's, the Club Lido, the Showman's Bar, the Club Harlem, the Baby Grand, and in occasional spectaculars at the Apollo Theatre, the Audubon and Renaissance ballrooms, Chateau Gardens, and many, many other places. It was a time when musicians were anxious to show off their style and facility, and for curious and extremely hip kids like Jackie McLean, there was a large opening into a world of awesome adventure: "I decided to be a jazz musician from the first time I took up the saxophone, around 1946. I wanted to be a doctor before that. When I heard Lester Young and Bird and Dexter and everybody, I decided. Of course I had my dream of what being a jazz musician was like. It would be like speeding along in a big car and passing a club with my name on the marquee. That's what I thought it was going to be about."

There was one particularly luminous star at Benjamin Franklin High School. Sonny Rollins was a senior when

Jackie was a freshman, and Jackie idolized him. Rollins was playing alto saxophone then, and Jackie played with him whenever and wherever they could find a place for a group to set up around a piano. Rollins sounded at that time like Coleman Hawkins playing alto, McLean like Lester Young. When Sonny Rollins graduated in 1947, Jackie transferred to Theodore Roosevelt High School, following another friend.

That friend was Andy Kirk, Jr., whose father had been an important bandleader since the early Twenties. He had worked with Mary Lou Williams, and had led a nationally famous band, "Andy Kirk and His Twelve Clouds of Joy," which was best known for the hit record "Until the Real Thing Comes Along." The younger Kirk was an exceptionally gifted student and Harlem's number-one child prodigy in music, rivaled only by Sonny Rollins. He is now one of those walking legends which the jazz world is so full of, but in the Forties Kirk was a young musician who commanded the respect, if not the awe, of everyone who heard him play. He could play any reed instrument and could read any music that could be put on paper. Jackie practiced with Kirk, and there was a great contrast in their playing because Jackie's tone already had the bite that still identifies him, while Kirk's tone was characterized by a delicate lightness.

The important thing was that, unlike McLean and Rollins, Kirk was already playing in the style of Charlie Parker. Jackie, who had been listening to Charlie Parker records ever since he had gone to work at his stepfather's record shop, was anxious to learn that kind of fingering, and to develop an ear oriented to rapid-fire improvisation around chord changes. To Jackie, by now old enough to rebel against going to church every Sunday and having to play in the Abyssinian Baptist band, Andy Kirk was a revelation. Kirk not only sounded like Charlie Parker, he had developed

Bird's ideas into a conception of his own, and had come along so fast that Bird even came to search him out every time he was in New York. Many musicians who were around at the time report that Andy Kirk, Jr., was enormously talented, and that the only two young reedmen who could play in his company without being shamelessly outclassed were Sonny Rollins and the youngest of them all, Jackie McLean.

When Jackie went into rehearsals with Kirk he had been playing and studying the alto saxophone for only a little more than a year, and Kirk, only a couple of years older than Jackie, assumed the role of teacher.

The emotional problems which Andy Kirk, Jr., endured during those years will not be discussed here. Suffice it to say that they were so overwhelming that he stopped playing music entirely before he was twenty years old, and has never picked up a saxophone again. Jackie, like many other Harlem musicians of the Forties, considers Kirk an authentic genius and feels that one of the supreme musical intelligences of the times dropped out of his era at a tremendous loss to the development of music in mid-twentieth-century America.

One day when he was playing Charlie Parker and Bud Powell records in his stepfather's record shop, a boy wearing coveralls, about a year younger than Jackie, came in to hear the latest jazz releases. He overheard Jackie expounding to someone in the store about pianist Bud Powell, and walked over and identified himself as Bud Powell's brother. Jackie, the hipster, didn't believe him, and asked the kid if he played piano. No? Then he couldn't be Bud Powell's brother. There was a long argument, and the kid in the coveralls stalked out, telling Jackie that his brother was in the hospital but would be out by the next Sunday, and then he'd be able to prove that Bud Powell was his brother. Sunday was fine with

Jackie, because he used to close the store early on that day and take a stack of records into the back room to practice from them.

The boy did come back on the appointed day, and Jackie closed up the store, not because he really believed that the boy would take him to meet Bud Powell, but because he wasn't going to take any chances. For a kid as hip as Jackie, Bud Powell was a greater figure than the President, and a few minutes with Bud Powell on Sunday would make great conversation at Roosevelt High on Monday. He closed the shop as soon as the kid came in, grabbed his saxophone case, and followed him out. They had to go only a block or so, just around the corner, up the stairs, and in to an over-stuffed couch in the living room. Two large French doors opened and: " 'My brother tells me you don't believe that I'm Bud Powell.' And so being sixteen years old and very inquisitive, I said, 'Well, like I said, I never saw Bud Powell. I only know Bud Powell by music, you know.' Very arrogant, like I knew I was into something. With this, Bud went to the piano and sat down; and there was no question. It was Bud. Then he told me to take out my horn, and I was scared to death. He asked me what did I know, and I called a Charlie Parker blues, 'Buzzy,' which I had just been practicing from the records. It was a gas." He and Bud grew close immediately, and Jackie became one of Bud's few interests.

Bud Powell had never been interested in the musical potential of his brother, and it was an excellent but now forgotten pianist named Bob Bunyan who taught Richie Powell chords on the piano. Richie would study with Bunyan, and then go home and watch his brother practice. Bud, for some reason, never showed him anything. Richie and Jackie became tight friends and used to rehearse together whenever Richie could take some time off from the High

School of Design, where he was a top student. By the mid-Fifties, Richie was establishing himself as one of the more talented composers and pianists of his generation when he died in the car accident which also killed the equally precocious trumpet player Clifford Brown.

The sessions with Bud became a regular thing with Jackie, and some critics have suggested that his rhythmic approach to alto playing came out of these sessions. Bud started out by teaching Jackie on paper, but then decided that Jackie's ear was more developed than his reading sense, and applied the more direct approach. Not only was Jackie learning, but lessons with Bud Powell were an unmatchable status symbol among the hipper students at Theodore Roosevelt High School.

This was a time when Harlem gangs were numerous and vicious, and one had either to be a member of a strong gang or exercise a very high level of diplomacy to get through high school without being regularly beaten. Jackie was a diplomat, and, to get them to leave him alone, he once convinced a particularly tough gang that he was Duke Ellington's son. One of Jackie's most cherished and invaluable high school friends was a Golden Gloves boxer named Skippy, and when Skippy challenged Jackie to take him up to Bud Powell's apartment to prove that he knew Bud, Jackie could not refuse. But he had no idea of the depth of Bud's feeling on the subject of visitors. He and Skippy went upstairs and made themselves comfortable in Bud's living room.

"Bud came out and right away looked at him and said, 'How dare you! Would I be doing that in your house!' Skippy didn't know what he was doing, he wasn't doing anything actually, and he said, 'Well, what did I do?' And Bud said, 'Would I sit in your house with my legs crossed? Get out!'

And Skippy left, dejected, and Bud stood in the corner and said, 'Never darken the portals of my abode again!' He spoke very dramatically, but it just fit in with the rest of his personality. It was a situation a lot like that when I heard Bud come out with a phrase, 'Captain of my ship and master of my soul,' and I thought it was an original Bud Powell. When he said it, it sounded like it just happened at the moment."

One day in 1948, Jackie accompanied Bud to a ballroom for an afternoon trio gig, on the same program with the blind British pianist George Shearing, who had just arrived in New York and had become an immediate sensation. Jackie went backstage with Bud just as Shearing was being escorted off.

"George was playing first, and Bud and I were in the wings, and when George Shearing was coming off, Bud walked up to him in the middle of the stage and collared him, and said something to the effect that 'You dare play before me.' George Shearing was not only not shaken up, but was cool about it. He said, like: 'Bud, it's an honor; I didn't know you were here.' And I was thinking, 'Damn Bud, that's kind of weird.'

"Bud started a tune, I'll never forget this, he turned around and looked at me and came walking off the stage, the rhythm section was still playing, he came up to me and looked down in my face with a lot of intensity and said, 'Jackie, I collared a blind man.' And he looked very concerned and upset about it, and then he turned and went back and played."

During their lessons, Bud did not teach Jackie harmony or theory, but worked specifically on his ear. He would call a tune, have Jackie play it, and play the chord changes behind Jackie until his student could improvise freely around those chord changes. One day Bud finally took him to Birdland and from the bandstand called him to come up and play. It was a great honor for a teen-ager, and Jackie has never forgotten it.

Jackie remembers a Sonny Rollins breakthrough that rocked all the young musicians around Harlem. Rollins had finished high school in 1947 and had dropped off the scene during the entire summer and autumn. His sound had been like a Coleman Hawkins on alto saxophone, but when he returned late in the winter of 1948, he was more like a Charlie Parker playing a tenor saxophone. The transition had Jackie thinking; he had heard Sonny Stitt playing bebop lines on tenor saxophone, and recognized the possibilities there. Now that Sonny Rollins had made the switch to tenor, Jackie wondered if he should not follow suit. He decided not to.

"Sonny [Rollins] influenced everybody uptown, playing every instrument. There were a lot of musicians in our neighborhood like [drummer] Arthur Taylor, [pianist] Kenny Drew, Connie Henry, who played bass for a while, Arthur Phipps, who also played bass, and [alto saxophonist] Ernie Henry, and there were guys who used to come from out of the neighborhood to see what was happening, like Walter Bishop. Sonny was the leader of all of them. And when Miles came to town he began to hang up there on the Hill with us."

In 1948, a blues tenor saxophonist named Charles Singleton met Jackie on the street and asked him about making a record. As a result, Jackie, on baritone saxophone with the Singleton orchestra, recorded a song which was a hit in black communities all over America, "Do the Camel Walk." The other side was a blues, "Hard Times Are Coming Baby," and Jackie says today that its title made it one of the most prophetic records he has ever made.

Rollins had a teen-age band, and they used to play all the West Indian dances and cocktail sips that they could find. The band included Rollins on tenor saxophone, Jackie, Lowell Lewis playing trumpet, Arthur Taylor on drums, Kenny Drew on piano, and either Percy Heath, Connie Henry, or Arthur Phipps on bass.

It was during this period that Jackie started using heroin. I have been told by several men who used heroin during the Forties that, looking back on their own experiences, there was a conscious attempt (most say by the Mafia) to create a market. The quality of the heroin available was markedly better than it is now, as it was cut much less than it is today, and the bags were considerably larger, so that it took less time to acquire a habit. Jackie, over the years, saw the bags diminish in size with the growing market, and the percentage of milk sugar in the heroin increase. There was heroin in the jazz set before it was on the street, and Jackie feels that this may have been the result of the all-pervasive influence of Charlie Parker. In that set, which Jackie admired so much, heroin was one of the greatest symbols of hipness. It was in this era that the idea of hip developed, and Jackie is one of the last of the original hip musicians. They created a language, a dress, a music, and a high which were closed unto themselves and allowed them to one-up the rest of the world. The bebop era was the first time that the black ego was expressed in America with self-assurance, and heroin, because its effect blocks out all doubt, is a drug that facilitates the self-assurance. There was heroin all around the hip teen-age set that Jackie ran with, and many of the idols whose music, speech, dress, whose every mannerism they were endeavoring to copy, were heroin addicts. The true giant of that era, easily the greatest American musician of his generation, Charlie Parker, was an addict. Many of the people who appear in these pages, in fact, have been narcotic addicts at some time during their lives, but most of them have, by now, like Jackie, stopped using heroin.

Jackie makes no excuses for becoming a drug addict, nor is it something that he's ashamed of. It was one of several sides of his life that caused him more pain than pleasure, and he does not consider having to get his pennies together to meet the connection any more distasteful or self-destructive than choosing to live with dishonest record companies, disrespectful nightclub owners, or a disinterested public that guaranteed only long periods of unemployment: "The first thing is, I didn't get involved with drugs because of any particular person. Nobody made me use them, and nobody influenced me to use them. And I don't think anybody ever does; I want to get that straight. A person uses drugs because like, you've got to get burnt before you know what fire is. I was warned about drugs by people on the outside, but I can't say that I really knew what was involved in it [heroin] when I started using it. I just thought it was something else that adults didn't want high school kids to do. Today drugs are brought down front more and kids are more aware of what drugs are than when I was coming up. When I was coming up it was known as 'banging' and I only knew it as something you did that was wrong. But as for knowing that it came from opium and reading as much literature on it as there is around today and having people trying to help the kids to stay away from it like they do today, that just wasn't happening when I was coming up. It was just another way of getting high, like drinking or smoking pot.

"I liked the high when I first started, but then it took over the whole mind and body and life. The thing I liked about the high was it relaxed me, as all opiates do. I understand that now. At the time I thought it was, like, this relaxes you; no stage fright; just go on and play. And of course when you're relaxed you play better. But for that minute you think the drug is making you play better, and you find out later on that you were just relaxed. Now, the opposite is what I need to play. I need to be stimulated from within. I don't need to be relaxed any more. I relaxed all those years that I was using narcotics, you know. It didn't do anything for me except teach me a long hard lesson, that's all."

Jackie has had to endure his share of do-gooders who think that to kick a heroin habit requires only a little more will power and a nice set of middle-class associates, and hard-liners who think that drug addicts should be isolated in concentration camps. He offers no apologies to either, since he feels no guilt: "I think that some people *should* be junkies. I don't think that I should have been a junkie, but I really think that some people should be tied down and in-jected with narcotics, especially the ignorant people who think they know all about it. The people who have so much to say about it and pass as authorities on it, I think that they're the ones that should have to live with it. Those that think that you can just kick it, it's in the mind, and those people that think all drug addicts are just useless and worth-less criminals and all that, I think that they ought to be tied to a tree and injected and left there and someone should come back and give them an injection every day until they're hooked and then cut the rope loose and see what they do to get their narcotics every day. Let them see if they can just stop, see if it's just in the mind.

"Actually, from my experience, I think there are more people in the medical profession using drugs than there are jazz musicians. That's because they have access to drugs and know what they will do. The average man will use drugs if he has access to them. You need some kind of crutch, liquor, pills, or something, to live in our society. When it was just a problem up in Harlem and it was just black people and Spanish people using drugs, nobody cared much about it because they've got plenty of room down at the Tombs, plenty of room on Riker's Island [two New York City jails]. All you've got to do is put them away. But now that it's getting out into Westchester County and the little heiresses are falling dead from overdoses and all kinds of well-to-do white people are getting involved in it, now people have decided to do something about it.

"Why *did* so many musicians use drugs? In the Forties, times were harder than they are now. It was right after the war, and the situation all over the country was pretty bad. Everyone had troubles, and heroin made you forget your troubles. It doesn't make your life too realistic, but it relaxes you and tends to take things off your mind, troubles, you know. It doesn't give you hallucinations and make you think the world is a bowl of cherries, but it does take your mind off your troubles.

"In the Forties it was just there, it was really being pushed on to the scene. A lot of musicians used it and a lot of teen-agers. Gangs were very big in the Forties, and most of the gang members went right into drugs right after they left the gang. From the frying pan into the fire. It was especially hard for musicians to exist in those days, so a lot of musicians sold themselves down the river under the influence of narcotics because they had to have that bit of money to get along."

Jackie regrets the disappearance of some facets of the music scene. He feels that the idea of music for its own sake was bigger in the Forties than it is now, when no one gives up any music without being paid for it. Jamming was the big thing in the Forties, and Jackie regrets its passage. As a teen-ager, he would sit in, in clubs where he was too young to be served a drink. There was a constant blend of the old and the new, and musicians who had just come to town had no trouble testing themselves in the litmus of the Harlem night-club scene. Minton's was *the* place, and the after-hours cabarets such as Monroe's Uptown House allowed for further jamming by all the musicians who got off work at four o'clock in the morning.

Jackie also regrets that there were so many fine musicians who, for whatever reasons, never made it past the neighborhood scene. Trumpeter Lowell Lewis was one, along with alto saxophonist Rudy Williams, and, of course, Andy Kirk, Jr., who was already one of the leading be-boppers before he finished high school. There were also pianists Herbie Nichols, Al Walker, and Bob Bunyan, one of the early Bud Powell followers. "So many men who had so much to contribute just never got the chance. Some of them went to jail, some died of overdoses, and some got married and took up day gigs to support their families."

There was a talented and completely ruined musician named Horsecollar* who was well known on The Hill in those days, Jackie remembers. Horsecollar chewed Benzedrine and was always very excited and full of ideas: "Most of the saxophone players from that era and from that area knew him, because Horsecollar was always walking around with his horn and taking it out to play. He'd come into a record store and people'd be listening to a record, trying to decide whether or not to buy it, and Horsecollar would take out his horn and play along with the record whether the people liked it or not. He was an eccentric. But when he came on The Hill we liked him up there because he could really play. I used to dig Horsecollar because he used to make a lot of

* No relation to Floyd "Horsecollar" Williams.

sense even though I knew he was crazy. He'd get off on tan-
gents about drum rhythms and notes that could sound like
voices and chattering of babies on the saxophone and all
kinds of things that I used to think were amusing but crazy,
you know; like, I believed him in a funny kind of way. It's
only in the last few years when I dug the kind of things that
guys are doing now that I got to understand what Horsecollar was talking about in those days."

One of the leaders who took the young Jackie under
his wing was Thelonious Monk. Monk's regular alto saxophonist at the Club 845 in the Bronx was the late Ernie
Henry, and when Henry was unavailable, Monk would call
Jackie: "Art Blakey was in that band, and Coleman Hawkins
was the tenor player. I was young and still not sure of myself, and it was a great experience working with Monk. I was
nervous, and when I would think that I was asked to play
by Monk it would give me the kind of encouragement that
I think young people need, going through that particular
period in their lives, playing for an audience for the first
time."

Monk is known for his idiosyncrasies, and Jackie got to
see all of them—he never knew what to expect from Monk.
One particular incident stands out clearly in Jackie's mind
as an example of Monk's whimsy: "Monk was working up at
the Audubon Ballroom, and I was working with him. During
the course of the evening, I mentioned that my mother had
made a chocolate pie, and Monk said that he wanted a piece
of it, so I said yeah, just passing it off, like, the next time my
mother makes a pie I'll call you up. But after the gig was
over I went downstairs and there was Monk waiting for me.
He said, "I'll walk you home, I'm going to get that pie." It
was about four o'clock in the morning, it was weird. I was
only seventeen years old, and my mother didn't really like

me to be out that late. I certainly couldn't have taken any
company up to the house for a piece of pie at that hour, so
I said, "Look.Monk, I can't have any company." And he said,
"Well, I don't need to be company, I can wait for it and you
can go in and get it and pass it out to me." So he walked all
the way across Harlem, up to the top of The Hill, came up
to the sixth floor, and stood in the hallway while I went
inside and cut a piece of chocolate pie and put it in a piece
of wax paper and passed it out to him. Then he thanked me
and went downstairs. That's the way it was with Monk: if
he wanted to do something, anything, he'd go on and do it."

On one occasion, Jackie had the privilege of having his
hero as a sideman. "I remember in 1950 I had a cocktail sip
to play. It was my quartet, and it paid twelve dollars for each
man. This was one of the few gigs that I had at that time
for my own group. I called Arthur Taylor for him to make it,
and asked him who I should get to play piano, and Arthur
Taylor said why don't you call up Monk? It was weird because I never thought of asking somebody that I admired as
much as I admired Monk, you know. I called up Monk and
he said he'd make it, and when I got to the gig that night
he was already there in his suit and tie and everything and
he worked all night and got his twelve dollars and left.

"In those days Monk was playing just when he wanted
to, more or less. But everybody was sleeping on [ignoring]
him except for the active jazz musicians and a few jazz fans
around them. That's why I get a little mad now when I hear
people expounding on Monk so much, because he has been
playing close to the same thing since I can remember. Monk
is one of the few musicians who you can go into the club
every night and hear, and he'll play the same tunes, and you
don't get tired of them or anything like that. I know I don't,
he's always surprising me."

Jackie feels that people have tended too much to regard Monk as a talented nut. During all his years of dealing with Monk, Jackie has found him to be enormously wise, lucid, and informed: "Monk is a deep person; I know this because I know Monk well. His interests vary far beyond what most people would imagine. He's very easy to know as long as you deal with him in a plain and friendly way. But if you try to be dishonest with him or play mental chess with him, then you might have trouble. His mind is something that should be respected at all times. People are too quick to think that a jazz musician knows jazz and that's it, you know.

"For example, if you asked Monk about the war in Vietnam, I'm sure that he could sum it up for you in a very few words. That's his style on piano as well as in talking: very few words. And I'm sure he could give you a short and reasonable solution. It might not be the one that this country would want to accept, but I'm sure it would save them millions of dollars. But if you asked Bud Powell, he might not even know about the war in Vietnam. I just don't think it's something that Bud would be interested in. They're both very deep men, but Monk is deep in a lot of areas where Bud is deep in himself. Bud does things like carry one of Bob Thompson's [Bob Thompson was a young black painter who died in June 1966 in Rome] small paintings around in his pocket with him all the time and taking it out and looking into it, I mean really *into* it, at various times."

Jackie also feels that Monk has deeper roots in folk tradition than most people realize: "Monk said to me that when he was young he first started playing piano with a church-type band, that he used to go out of town traveling with the sanctified band that played spirituals and things, but that these things had a very strong rhythm, as you know. I know what he means about the rhythm, because if you go to a sanctified church it's impossible to sit there, if you've got any rhythm in you, without something happening. Even if you hold it back and say, well, I'm going to be cool and enjoy it from within, it's hard to keep still and sit there because it'll get you one way or another. When I was very young I used to go to visit my grandmother in North Carolina sometimes, and she would take me and my cousins to her church, which was sanctified. We would be sitting there giggling at the people who would be jumping on the side; they'd go down to the middle and get in front and jump and go into their different things. But when my grandmother would give us a look and we would have to get ourselves together and forget about giggling and just be listening, it would get to us and we'd all feel like jumping too.

"With Monk it was the same. You can still hear traces of those roots in his music today. If you listen to Monk's sounds and his rhythm, then you can still hear that old sanctified influence. It's not like he got his sound out of nothing."

One of Jackie's favorite avocations during his teen-age years was following his heroes around. One of his favorites was Dexter Gordon, and what follows was the kind of event that Jackie regarded as a coup: "I used to love Sonny Stitt on alto (I love him on tenor now), and I remember going one Sunday afternoon to Lincoln Square [an old ballroom that was on the site of the present Lincoln Center complex] to hear him. I was too young and too young-looking to get in —I had on dark glasses and a hat, trying to make it, but I couldn't—and the guy at the door refused me. I started to walk away, but I saw Dexter Gordon coming down the street, and I ran up to him and told him the situation. Dexter recognized me as the little pest who played alto saxophone, and said, "Give me your money, man, and I'll take you in." I gave him my $1.50, and I went in as his cousin. That gave me a very proud feeling as I walked by the guy who had refused me."

Lincoln Square was a large dancehall which was used for several different kinds of functions. Paul Robeson, for example, had spoken at one of several political rallies held there in the Thirties. In the Forties there were numerous Lincoln Square dance-concerts, and the program that Jackie went to see that Sunday was typical of the kind of affair that one could attend at the time.

"I'll tell you who was on the bill that day. Art Blakey, Kenny Clarke, Max Roach, Ben Webster, Dexter Gordon, Sonny Stitt, Red Rodney, Charlie Parker, and Miles Davis. But Miles didn't even play with Bird on that set. Bird was playing with Ben Webster and Dexter Gordon and Freddie Webster on trumpet. Fats Navarro was playing with Sonny Stitt. Miles was playing with Bud. All this in one day.

"It was a lot like the functions they have now at Town Hall and Carnegie Hall and sometimes Lincoln Center, where you see programs like the [March, 1966] John Coltrane program with the Titans of the Tenor Saxophone, but only then it was given in a dancehall atmosphere. You could bring up folding chairs—they had rows of folding chairs close to the bandstand and near the back, away in the back, there was an open area to pass around in. People could dance in the back if they wanted to, but most people used to take their folding chairs and move them up near the front to be near the music. That's what they were there for, not for dancing. I had just started to play then, and I didn't really know the difference between swing and bebop. Skippy Williams was the intermission band then, and he's a guy who never made it big, but he always kept a boss little band at that time. You can hear him today up at Beefsteak Charlie's. I heard Sonny Stitt, and then I heard Freddie Webster, and then I heard Skippy Williams. Then Bird came in, and they played 'Cottontail.' I'll never forget that, man, like they played as soon as he came in. I think that's the first time I ever felt the true influence of Charlie Parker. Charlie Parker overwhelmed me. And I sat with my mouth open listening to Dexter Gordon, too. Ben Webster was on the set, and that was his famous solo on Duke's version of 'Cottontail,' which he played with Bird, and it was beautiful. Kenny Clarke was the drummer and Klook was as hip then as he is now."

Charlie Parker, Bud Powell, Thelonious Monk, Dizzy Gillespie, and the others had by now moved downtown to the famous 52nd Street aggregation of nightclubs, and they made only rare appearances at the ballrooms and theaters of Harlem. In a way, it was a lucky thing for Jackie, as he had to be home by ten o'clock at night and therefore could not catch any of the nightclub shows. He could, and did, however, play hooky from school to catch the shows at the theaters: "I first heard Max Roach with Dizzy's big band when they were playing at the McKinley Theatre in the Bronx, and Charlie Parker was in that band with either Tommy Potter or Curly Russell on bass and Freddie Webster, Kenny Dorham, and Fats Navarro on the trumpets, and Henry Pryor was one of the alto players. Lucky Thompson was in the tenor section, Leo Parker was playing baritone, and J. J. Johnson was in the trombone section. That was a hell of a band.

"But even though we used to go to see the band, there were some other things in the stage show that I remember just as clearly and that we enjoyed just as much. The dancers, Patterson and Jackson, for example. They were two big fat cats who were very light on their feet, and they always had some other kind of routine that went along with their dancing. It was a comedy routine, but they were really great dancers too.

"I remember that I saw them again at the Apollo when I went to see Bird with his five pieces around 1948, the year Kirk graduated from high school. When Bird was at the Apollo, we would go early in the morning, and stay and watch the show all day long. We would watch him from the first show until after three o'clock, when it was time to go home from school. We used to go home and put our books up, and then tell our parents that we were going to the Apollo, and they'd let us go and we'd split and go and watch Bird again until nine, when it was time to go home at night. We'd run out and get some hot dogs at intermission, and that would be all we had to eat all day long. Kirk knew Bird and introduced me to him. Bird had heard him play quite a few times, and used to come and look him up whenever he could."

Jackie had met Charlie Parker long before through Bud Powell, but Jackie was just starting to play the saxophone at that first meeting, and didn't have enough confidence in his playing to approach Bird as a musician. Now, however, after a couple of years of study with Bud Powell, and after acquiring some reputation as one of the young prodigies on the alto saxophone, he was only too glad to introduce himself as a musician. "We used to run around when the picture was on and see if we could catch Bird coming out and talk to him and hang outside and then run back for the show. We did this for the whole week that he was there."

Jackie's first job after his high school graduation in 1949 was at the Paramount Theater where large music shows were often produced. His mother had told him that she wouldn't be content with his "just laying around all day, living the life of a musician, until I really could live the life of a musician by playing for money. She told me to get a job and bring some home." Jackie took two friends from his neighborhood, went down to the theater, and insisted that they be hired together. They were the first black ushers at the Paramount Theater.

"I don't want to seem snobbish, but most of the mothers on the Hill made it a point to give their children good manners and all that. So we all had good manners, but we were all hip junkies too. It was pretty ridiculous. We all had habits, and they expected us to stand at attention and do the military thing in that monkey suit that they gave you at the Paramount. We had to have our nails clean, and it's very hard for a junkie to have clean nails, especially young junkies. And we were young and rebellious junkies from uptown, and there we were ushering in monkey suits at the Paramount. But even though I never got to hear Bird there, I was very lucky, because Teddy Hill was on the bill for one week, and Duke Ellington was on the bill for the next. I only lasted two weeks."

I asked Jackie what kind of scene 52nd Street was then, and he said it was "... like walking along the boardwalk at Coney Island. On 52nd Street you passed from one club to the other, and there was something happening at every club. You might pass one door and see Don Byas and Dizzy Gillespie; you reach the next door and it's Miles and Charlie Parker, Max [Roach] and [pianist] Duke Jordan and [bassist] Tommy Potter, and you go down to the next place and you see like Coleman Hawkins and [trumpeter] Charlie Shavers, and across the street there would be Art Tatum and Erroll Garner on the same bill. Then you'd go down to the next place, and there might be some girls stripping. You know, it was, like, you just moved from place to place. I remember one time on 52nd Street Dizzy and his big band were in one club, across the street it was Coleman Hawkins and Don Byas, and down the street was Bird, and at another club on the street was Tadd [Dameron, a major pianist and composer of the period] and Fats [Navarro, the great trumpeter]. But then, it didn't seem like it sounds now because you'd ride down to 52nd Street and run into somebody you knew and say, "Who's on the block?" you know. And they'd say, "Oh well, Fats, Tadd, Bird, Diz's big band, and Coleman Hawkins and Art Tatum." And you'd just keep moving. But now, to find all that, or to find anything close to that, in any area, in any town, anywhere on this planet, would be impossible. What made it more interesting for me was that I couldn't go in any of the clubs because I was too young, so I stayed outside, moving from one door to another, until the doorman would run me away, but I mostly hung around where Bird was playing because I knew Bird would come out at intermission and I'd get a chance to talk to him, and any kind of exchange of words with him was enough inspiration for me to go home and practice the horn for a month. That used to gas me.

"One night Bird invited us in. Me and my friend Jelly, who played clarinet, went inside. He's dead now, but we used to hang out together then. Bird went in at nine o'clock, played one tune, and the club was empty. We had our faces pressed against the window at the door, and he came down after the tune was over and told the doorman to let us in and give us a coke. We sat down and he asked us what we wanted to hear and we told him 'Night in Tunisia,' and he went up and played it. That's the kind of cat he was. Then he told us we had to split after the tune was over.

"I remember one time at the Royal Roost, I went down there with Jelly, and this time we got in because we moved our age up. We got to the table, and we didn't have enough money to pay for our bill. We told Bird about it, and Bird spoke to the manager and told him not to throw us out or make any scene because we had told him that we were waiting for Jelly's big brother to bring down the difference in the money."

I asked pianist Bob Bunyan about 52nd Street, and his view was quite different. Bunyan, more than five years older than Jackie, was already trying to make a living at jazz in those days, while Jackie at the time was concerned with music only for the sake of music. Bunyan remembers seeing Bud Powell, Thelonious Monk, Charlie Parker, Dizzy Gillespie, and others trying to show the younger musicians new chord changes and new rhythmic patterns. The older musicians were used to very tight chords, tightly arranged, and they would complain that the younger cats played so much of the chord that there was nothing left for them to play. The jobs on 52nd Street, as everywhere else in New York, were hotly contested, and as the older group had control of the hiring, the new musicians had to be well-versed in the old swing style to be employed. Rollins and Jackie McLean, recalls Bunyan, were still living with their families; they didn't have to hustle for the jobs or compromise their music by playing patterns that they believed to be outdated. But those musicians for whom music was a livelihood had no choice if they wanted to work. The fight between the old and the new was a very real matter for Bunyan, since jobs were at stake.

It is vivid in Bunyan's memory that it was the white musicians who received the biggest push from the industry in this battle for jobs. *Down Beat* and *Metronome* magazines would give them enormous space, and it was a bitter complaint among the black musicians that these magazines would never put a Negro on their covers. Considering the number and the vitality of the musicians who were coming out of Harlem, Bunyan feels that George Auld, Serge Chaloff, Brew Moore, Allen Eager, and Stan Getz received more than their fair share of the jobs. Most hired all white sidemen, and commanded much more of the showbill than their talents deserved in the midst of so much black genius.

Before long, the buildings on 52nd Street that housed the jazz clubs were renovated or torn down altogether, and the entire jazz scene moved around the corner to Birdland, which took its name from Charlie Parker's long residence there.

Meanwhile, Jackie was solidifying his reputation as one of the most virulent young beboppers in New York. He had become a close friend of Miles Davis, and when Miles hit town two days before he was scheduled to open at Birdland, he asked Jackie to assemble a group for him. Jackie called bassist Connie Henry and pianist Gil Coggins. Coggins was from Jackie's neighborhood, and, as one of the greatest piano accompanists of the era, he fit perfectly into Miles's blue lyric style.

The first time Jackie played with Miles at Birdland, he was so nervous that he vomited between the bandstand and the men's room. He was nineteen and still impressionable enough to feel shaky about playing in the most famous jazz room in the world in front of the very musicians he had been admiring for years. Men like Fats Navarro and Dexter Gordon sat in with the group from time to time, and on these occasions Jackie was so nervous that he wanted to leave. Then one day, when Charlie Parker sat in with Miles, Jackie played "fours" with him. He was never nervous again.

Jackie and Miles, who had known each other since 1949, continued to be good friends, and even roomed together on 21st Street between Sixth and Seventh avenues: "I looked up to Miles, and he helped me in a lot of areas. He was the same way he is now. People say that Miles has gotten arrogant since he became successful, but Miles was arrogant when his heels didn't point in the same direction. I learned a lot from him, both on and off the bandstand. You might say that I was in the University of Miles Davis. I remember once when he got after me about a tune that I didn't know; the tune was 'Yesterdays,' and I passed it off by saying that I was young, like, I'll learn it before I die. Miles cursed me out so bad, and he could really curse, that I never used that excuse again."

At nineteen, Jackie made a record with Miles Davis, Sonny Rollins, Walter Bishop, Tommy Potter, and Art Blakey, all of whom by then had been associates of his for many years. That record was *Dig* (on the Prestige label), and it has since come to be regarded as a modern jazz classic. *Dig* was one of Miles Davis' first recordings as a leader; and since *Dig*, over forty records have been issued under his name. *Dig* represented a breakthrough for Miles, because it was the first recording that he had made that was produced specifically for LP release. The two that preceded *Dig* are listed in the current catalogue as *Birth of the Cool* (on Capitol) and *Early Miles* (on Prestige), the former a record of mint historical importance, as its overorganization and prismic harmonies are generally considered to be the formal beginning of the cool movement in jazz.

With *Dig*, the LP emerged in jazz as a form in itself. Soloists were for the first time able to play more than one chorus, which allowed them to approximate nightclub performances far more closely than they had been able to do in the past. Since *Dig*, many musicians have exploited the LP as a medium, and some even have used the entire record to perform one piece. In *Dig*, there is a spontaneity that is a clear result of this opportunity to record more extended performances than musicians had been accustomed to in recording sessions.

Dig, besides being Jackie McLean's recording debut, was a near-debut for Sonny Rollins and Walter Bishop. All come out of this recording extremely well. Rollins plays with a surprising amount of individuality, retaining, as he did, a large heavy tone when most of his contemporaries were trying to espouse the silken sounds of the Lester Young–Stan Getz school of tenor-playing. Jackie displays a tone that is distinctively jagged but effective—he is justified in his pride at being one of the most easily recognizable alto saxophonists now playing jazz. His phrases retain a certain amount of separation—his ideas did not flow together as easily in *Dig* as they do today—and this may be interpreted either as a sign of immaturity or as a sign of Jackie's separateness from his most apparent *guru*, Charlie Parker.

Jackie made two other recordings with Miles Davis: one in 1952 with J. J. Johnson, Gil Coggins, Oscar Pettiford on bass, and Kenny Clarke on drums. Jackie does little on the first recording (it was part of a two-volume set on Blue Note) except to perform certain orchestral functions and play an occasional chorus. The other, with the Miles Davis All-Star Sextet/Quintet, including Percy Heath, Milt Jackson on vibes, Ray Bryant on piano, and Arthur Taylor on drums, was recorded in 1956; here, Jackie's phrases are even more independent than before, but at the same time they show that his ideas had expanded even further, and that he had refined his tone so that some of the edge had come off it to make for a more full-bodied sound. In these recordings Jackie emerges as a superior composer in the neo-bop idiom, and all three of the tunes that Miles selected for these dates have become jazz standards (Jackie was immensely proud to catch Coleman Hawkins at Birdland playing his "Donna," a tune he had written when he was still in his teens). Miles had recorded "Dr. Jackle" and "Minor March" more than once, and "Dr. Jackle" was one of the standards of Miles's most accomplished group, the great quintet that included John Coltrane. It is an elegant example of neo-bop writing at its best, showing as it does Jackie's concern with structuring a melody along rhythmic lines that then become the carriers of the melody, opening it into an ever-broadening expanse of possibility.

Jackie's work with Miles Davis projected him immediately into the forefront of alto saxophonists, solidified his reputation among jazz musicians as a proficient and imaginative composer and improviser, and introduced him favorably to the jazz public at large. Nonetheless, he has never been satisfied with any of the recordings he has made with Miles Davis; he feels that his performances in the clubs were much more electric than the recordings, and that he should have waited until he was more mature to record with Davis. Whether or not this is true, on the basis of the only recordings with Davis, Jackie McLean became a nationally known musician at the age of twenty.

Jackie's family thought that the climate of the college campus might be more salubrious than the jazz life for the kid who had been an addict for more than three years. He had relatives in North Carolina, and North Carolina Agricultural and Technical College was decided on as the best place for him to matriculate; the school was known for a music department that had trained several of the leading band directors throughout the Southern school systems. But Jackie was far too hip for the college campus and could find very little to relate to in Greensboro, North Carolina. He was full of stories about Charlie Parker and Miles Davis in Birdland, but who could he tell them to? It must be remembered that the South in 1952 was far more culturally isolated than it is now; records that were popular in New York often took years to get there. The students in Roosevelt High in New York had been far more cognizant of bebop music than those he found at N.C.A. & T. Campus activities, which he could not conceive of participating in, such as cutting the hair of freshmen and being recruited by fraternities, made him feel ridiculous. His way of thinking was completely at odds with the entire university structure. What to do, who to play music with, who to talk with, became insoluble problems, and he had to deal with the rigid segregation of the South for the first time since his preadolescent journeys there. Jackie returned to New York after one year at A. & T., and took up where he left off. He searched out all the jazz that he could find in "The Apple," and jammed with everyone who would let him.

One night, at a party in the Bronx, Jackie met Clarice Simmons. Dolly, as she was known, was unlike most of the other women he knew; she was from a strict West Indian family, and totally unaccustomed to jazz musicians and to the jazz life. For one thing, she had never seen a junkie, and when she noticed one sitting in the corner with his head on his chest, apparently asleep, but still following the conversation and occasionally contributing to it in a slow and throaty voice, she thought it an odd and fascinating thing. They were married in 1954, with Jackie assuming the responsibility for the two young children whom she had had by a previous marriage. Meanwhile, he had been taking on whatever jobs he could find, working at the Copa City with Paul Bley and later moving into the Cafe Bohemia with Pianist George Wallington.

The conflict between living the jazz life and rearing a family was getting to be a massive strain on Jackie, who could never be assured of a steady and permanent income. When a leading record company offered him a contract, he jumped at the first offer they made. He considers it one of the greatest mistakes he has ever made: "If you can imagine being under the Nazi regime and not knowing it, then you've got an idea of what it's like to be with that company. I was starving when I signed that contract. The baby was being born, so I was glad to get my name on a record and make some money. And my condition didn't help either; any money was money then. Everybody made that move—Miles was with that company, Sonny Rollins, John Coltrane, and Monk. They all got out of it as soon as they could, just as I did."

"It's a perfect example of giving everything and getting nothing back. They give you a little bit of front money, and then they tell you about the royalties you are going to get after the record is released. I did a million dates for them, and all it amounted to is that I paid for the whole thing: engineers, the notes on the back of the album, the color photograph, the whole thing, out of my money. I still get statements saying that I owe that company ridiculous sums like $50,000; I'm exaggerating, but it's not much less ridiculous than that.

"The record companies today are aware of what the cat's problems are. If they weren't aware that there aren't many jazz clubs going and that record dates are a necessity to many musicians and that some musicians use drugs, there would be more jazz musicians around with money. Certainly the record companies are making money on the jazz that they produce. They're not signing anybody with any company that's not making money. They're not making records for the sake of Allah, they're making records to make money.

But all they ever do when you go to them and ask them for some money you figure you've got coming to you, they just tell you that things are bad, that this or that album didn't do too good."

Jackie isn't positive how many records he actually made for the firm, but he estimates their number at more than twenty. He left the company in 1959 and has signed with Blue Note, with whom he makes a new contract every two years.

In 1956, Jackie joined Charlie Mingus' Jazz Workshop, for him the beginning of a new musical education. Mingus is a notoriously demanding leader and was one of the most adventurous composers of the late Fifties. Jackie's first contact with Mingus had been during that first 1951 record date with Miles Davis. Mingus had come to the studio with Miles that day, carrying his bass on his back, and stood at the piano, running over the tunes. It was Mal Waldron who made the introduction in 1956; Waldron was already working with the Jazz Workshop and was known to be a developing pianist and composer. Mingus already had been familiar with Jackie's work.

The Jazz Workshop was designed to be experimental, and during the course of its existence, Mingus gave advanced training to the most promising musicians he could find. The outstanding record that came out of the Workshop was the famous *Pithecanthropus Erectus*. According to Mingus, there were three interrelated ideas that he was trying to develop with the Workshop and with this record. One was the formulation of a system of composition in which the musicians could get a better idea of what he wanted from them than they could if he had simply written the ideas out on paper. To do this, he played out what he called the "framework" of the piece on the piano, both to demonstrate what he wanted in the way of feeling and interpretation and to give the musicians a familiarity with the chordal progression. The second idea was to enhance the individual expression of the musicians by giving them a context and a set of options that would permit maximum freedom within the necessary limits of group playing. To this end, Mingus set up different rows of notes for each musician against each chord, but left it to the musician to decide which of these notes he wanted to use. Thirdly, *Pithecanthropus Erectus* was intended to be a programmatic record, with three of its four tunes musically descriptive of particular situations. The title tune was intended to describe the development, psyche, and eventual downfall of the first man to stand erect; "A Foggy Day" used an old standard to picture the sights and sounds that one is likely to encounter in San Francisco; and "Profile of Jackie" is a ballad Mingus wrote to show Jackie McLean off in his most characteristic light.

If Jackie believed that he attended the University of Miles Davis, then Mingus' Jazz Workshop must have been his graduate seminar. The Workshop provided him with a great amount of exposure, both to the highly developed mind of Charles Mingus and to the work of some other men who had been trying to integrate jazz ideas with developments in modern classical music. Mingus had conceived the idea of a jazz workshop in the early Forties when he was attending Los Angeles City College, where there was such a workshop for classical composers. He first applied the concept in a series of Jazz Workshop concerts in Brooklyn in 1953, when he got a group of jazz musicians together to play each other's new work and to try out new ideas. (The Jay and Kai two-trombone quintet, led jointly by J. J. Johnson and Kai Winding, was an outgrowth of one of these concerts.) The original Jazz Workshop later turned into a Composers' Workshop, which included composer-performers Teddy Charles, John LaPorta, and Teo Macero, and was more involved with classical forms than with jazz. Almost all of the music in this group was written, and there was little room for free improvisation. It was in reaction against the rigidity of the Composers' Workshop that Mingus formed the second Jazz Workshop, in which formal notation was avoided as much as possible.

Jackie says that he came to Mingus "fixed in my ideas and set in my ways. I was strictly from bebop, and knew that was the way it had to be." Mingus set out immediately to break down the laws that Jackie had been playing by since he had first heard Charlie Parker and Sonny Rollins. "But Mingus wanted something else," said Jackie, "he wanted Jackie, and he used to tell me that. He said, 'I don't want Charlie Parker, man, I want Jackie.' Some nights he would be pleased, and he would tell me, 'Tonight you were playing Jackie, and that's what I want.' And on other nights he would tell me, 'Tonight I want Johnny Hodges,' and I had to go out and listen to Johnny Hodges and try to get what Mingus wanted out of Hodges' melodic idea; and that's when I got to appreciate how Hodges could express a certain feeling in a song. Since I couldn't vibrate, I had to do it with a Johnny Hodges concept coming through myself.

"I hadn't been content with what I was doing with changes yet, and here came Mingus telling me, 'Forget changes and forget about what key you're in,' and 'all notes are right,' and things like that, and it kind of threw me. I was going through a hip phase then, but I find that I really got involved with Mingus and all of his things on a lot of nights. Mingus gave me my wings, more or less; Mingus made me feel like I could go out and explore because he was doing it and was accepted by the audience and loved for it. He gave me my exploration papers. Writingwise, I wrote some of my most involved things then, things that stand up with what's happening today. I wrote 'Quadrangle' and 'Fickle Sonance' around that time."

The Workshop toured extensively, and Jackie was given some national in-person exposure for the first time. He was replaced, along with tenor saxophonist J. R. Montrose, in April, 1956 by tenor saxophonist Joe Alexander and trumpeter Bill Hardman.

Two months later, Jackie took Hank Mobley's seat with Art Blakey's Jazz Messengers, and stayed with the Messengers for two years. Jackie considers Art Blakey one of the most punctilious leaders in the jazz scene, and the fact that the Messengers are one of the most frequently employed groups in the jazz circuit was a much-needed boost for the morale of Jackie's family.

Jackie said: "I think Art Blakey is one of the finest bandleaders morally for a young musician, as far as sticking with a young man and making him feel secure on the road and feel secure working with his band is concerned. Today things are different than when I was coming up. If Art ever approached me and told me that he had a bill to pay and that my salary would be short by about maybe thirty or forty dollars for a week or two, I could continue to work and not feel funny. Today you give the musicians anything like that and they want to quit the band. The whole thing is different today, but I guess that's good business. When I was coming up, everybody was beating the bandleaders so bad that it was taken for granted. I guess somebody had to make the stand. The young kids coming up today make a stand, and they make the bandleaders make a stand."

Since Jackie is essentially a rhythm player, Blakey fit well into the requirements of his development. For example, one habit that he had picked up from Miles Davis was stand-ing next to the drummer and building his solos around the drummer's inflections. Jackie tends to play with a one/three inflection, and Blakey always played a two/four. This dif-ference was easily resolved with the Messengers, however, as Blakey plays so much besides the two/four. Jackie does feel that a lot of younger drummers made a mistake in emu-lating Blakey, as his patterns can be restrictive to a lesser talent. He finds that Roy Haynes's and Max Roach's influ-ences better fit the needs of the contemporary jazz drummer.

Jackie had by now made some records as a leader, and the critical response to them was getting better with every release, as exemplified by two reviews written by Nat Hentoff in *Down Beat* magazine in 1956. The first was a re-view of *Jackie McLean, Volume I* (on Ad Lib Records): "McLean's problem is twofold. He plays with drive, heated emotion, and a good beat. But he is still so much involved with his strong Bird influence that he has not thus far found his own voice and style. The second problem is cohesiveness. His choruses contain intriguing fragments but rarely hang together as a developed organic entity . . . but McLean plays with a lot of guts and that's good to hear these days."

Hentoff awarded that record four and one-half out of a maximum of five stars in the magazine's rating system; he was obviously pleased to find a musician playing such good hard blues in the face of the commercial dominance in the mid-Fifties by the cut-and-dried playing of the West Coast musicians. Hentoff's second review (of *Lights Out* on Pres-tige, with Elmo Hope, Doug Watkins, Arnold Taylor, and Donald Byrd) found ". . . an unflaggingly exciting outing . . . McLean [is] suddenly . . . maturing. His solos have gained in cohesion while losing none of the stripped-down emotion he always propels. . . . This, gentlemen, is jazz."

If 1956 saw a major breakthrough for Jackie McLean, 1955 had been the end of an era for him. Charlie Parker died in that year, and much of Jackie's life and vision of the world and music had been involved with Charlie Parker. It was after hearing Parker, after all, that Jackie McLean had first decided that the alto saxophone was an instrument worthy of study. It was Parker who had encouraged him and given him confidence as a musician; and, though Jackie does not blame Parker for his becoming a drug addict, he does feel that the Bird image was so extensive that many musicians turned to drugs as an unconscious emulation of the master.

Jackie says that he worshipped Bird as "a god, or as a parent, at least." He felt that nothing Bird could have done to him really could have upset him, as he regarded every touch of Parker's as a favor. The one exception would have been "If he had put me down musically. I don't think I could have stood that at the time that I was around Bird, because I worshipped him too much." As for the music: "I used to wait for Bird's records to come out to find something to play. Now when I listen to Bird it's more or less to reminisce, but still I get musical ideas from Bird. I don't think anybody went beyond Bird. I think cats are playing as much as Bird played as far as speed and things like that are concerned, but I don't think that anybody ever delved as far into the chordal aspect of jazz and change-based improvisation as Bird did."

There was one incident that occurred in 1950 of which he is particularly proud, as it was a concrete affirmation of the eighteen-year-old Jackie as a musician: "Bird called up my house and asked me if I wanted to play a gig for him. He had two gigs on the same date, one he was going to leave early to make the other one. The first was an afternoon thing upstate; the other was a night thing, a dance at the Chateau Gardens right down here on Houston Street. I said, 'Yeah, glad to.' To show you what kind of man he was, he said, 'Well, let me speak to your mother; I'll find out if it's cool.' And he spoke to my mother, and he asked if it would be all right and she said it was okay. I went down and played from about nine-thirty until eleven-thirty. Walter Bishop and Percy Heath were in the rhythm section; I don't remember who was on drums. Bird had two rhythm sections that night, one was with him upstate and one for the band I was in that was waiting for him downtown.

"Anyway, I remember at about eleven-thirty seeing the crowd of people rush to the door of the Chateau Gardens (it was a big place like the old Lincoln Square); I knew it was him by the noise they made when he stepped through the door. I can remember seeing people surround Bird, like thirty, forty, or fifty people deep, with him in the middle with just enough room to move toward the bandstand, everyone around him escorting him up, like, all the kids screaming and hollering.

"That was one of the biggest musical honors of my life, when Bird asked me. I played for him a couple of times. And that night when the gig was over he paid me, and that was an honor too, because I wasn't playing for money. I hadn't even thought of it when he asked me. I never asked him how much was the gig, and I didn't ask him at the end of the gig. I was just hanging around when he came over, you know, to ride uptown with him, and he called everybody one at a time, and then he called me and he said, 'Put your hand out,' and he started counting, putting dollar bills in my hand. When he got to eighteen, I still had my hand out and he said, 'Well damn, Jackie, take your hand back sometime.' So I took fifteen dollars and gave him three dollars back. That was a lot of money for me then."

Money was always a problem with Charlie Parker, and

it was a common practice of his to walk up to Jackie McLean, put his hand in Jackie's pocket, and take out whatever money was there. "The first time he did that, I had six dollars, and he took four and asked me if I could make it on a deuce, and one of my friends who was with me cracked up. I said, yeah, I could make out on a deuce. The next time I saw him, he reached into my pocket and I was broke, and I thought to myself, 'Well, this cat's going to be in for a surprise this time.' But he was putting something in. He put ten dollars into my pocket. That's the kind of guy he was. He used to do that to a lot of musicians. [Pianist] Freddie Redd is another person he played that pocket game with. When he reached into your pocket you didn't know whether you were going to blow or whether you were going to cop."

Stories of Charlie Parker's idiosyncrasies are legion, and there are more than a few people who have felt the sting of Bird's ire when they tried to patronize him. Jackie feels that Parker's bad-man reputation is one-sided. He knew Bird, like Monk, to be a broadly knowledgeable man who dealt easily with all kinds of people as long as he was approached in an honest and straightforward manner. "Bird could talk with the children and he could talk with your mother, and from conversations I saw him in with very well-educated people on all kinds of matters, you would think that Bird had a couple of college degrees. But he didn't, he just read a lot."

Parker always considered Jackie McLean a protégé of his, and one evening in 1952, when McLean was playing at Birdland with Miles Davis, Parker loudly applauded McLean's solos in an effort to get the other musicians present at the club to take notice of him. McLean said, "I know, because there was not much other applause. When I was through with the set, he rushed over and gave me a kiss on the neck."

Jackie told jazz writer Bob Reisner: "Sometimes, when we got through jamming at a small club, there were many musicians crowding around or sitting nearby, but he would pass his horn to me as a gesture that he wanted me to continue. We took walks, and I remember him, looking at a plane and saying how nice to be free of the earth, or standing in front of a fish store, admiring the light on the scales of the fish, creating color. He told me to emulate the straight cats. . . . One day he suggested that we go to the funeral parlor and see Hot Lips Page, who was laid out there. The place was empty. Bird stood a long time before the body, finally saying, 'Damn, his big wig sure looks good.' "

During the periods when he was using heroin, Charlie Parker always had difficulty keeping his horn out of the pawnshop. New Selmer-brand alto saxophones bring an easy forty or fifty dollars from the pawnshops, so that the instruments become security against the day when the addict-musician cannot earn or borrow enough money to keep his habit going. Jackie says that when Bird was at the Three Deuces, the owners used to keep his alto saxophone locked up, and gave it to him only when he came to work, taking it back every evening. Often when Parker had no horn, he would borrow Jackie's; and on two occasions he pawned Jackie's horn. Both incidents stand out in Jackie's mind for different reasons, and the horn itself was the least of it. Dolly and Jackie explained one incident:

DOLLY: "The first time I saw Charlie Parker was at a costume party. When I walked in I saw him sitting on a couch, and he frightened me. He had on a pair of pants that fell below his stomach, and they were cut off at the knee, and he had all this white paint on his chest and on his belly and some special thing around his bellybutton and on his face."

JACKIE: "He was supposed to be a Mau Mau."

DOLLY: "I don't know, but he frightened me, and he was drunk. Then someone introduced him to me, and I didn't know quite what to say to him.

"The second time I met him was at the Open Door, and that night I didn't have too much to say to him because he had pawned Jackie's horn, and I was very angry over the whole thing. It annoyed me because Jackie was very playful with him, and I couldn't understand why he should want to be friendly with Bird when he had just pawned Jackie's horn. We were with these other musicians, and Bird tried to get into the Open Door. For some reason, the owner of the Open Door didn't want to have jazz there anymore. But Bird wanted to play, and he told us, 'You all come with us, with me and Jackie.' Bird asked the owner to please let him play, but the guy didn't want to hear it. So we went to that place on Christopher Street off Seventh Avenue, Arthur's, and he literally had to talk the man into allowing him to play. You know, he had to beg him: 'Oh, just let me play a little while.' You know, this sort of thing. The drummer who was with us the man just refused to let into the place; he told Bird that the others could come in but that the little guy, the drummer, he wouldn't let him in. So we all went in, and Bird began to play, and after he played a little while, he brought Jackie up to play. He came and sat at the table, and he started talking to me about Jackie and telling me how good he sounded, and to sort of watch him and see that he continued to play, because from what he could hear, Jackie was one of the few people around who had anything to offer on the alto.

"But then he got kind of depressed. As we were leaving, we got outside and he told Jackie to kick him in the ass, because, he said, 'Here I am begging pennies for drinks, begging people to buy drinks for me, and putting myself down. And here I am begging people to let me play. I am Charlie

Parker, and I have to beg people to let me play. Kick me Jackie, and don't you ever allow this to happen to you.' It was very sad."

JACKIE: "I had to mock-kick him. It was very embarrassing; we were right in front of the club, and there were lots of people standing around. Even passers-by recognized Bird, because when he walked around the Village he was like a god. But he was very insistent that I plant my foot directly on his buttocks, right there in front of the club. He had a very deep voice and he was saying very loud, 'Kick me in my ass.' Like, he spoke very proper, he said, 'Jackie McLean, I want you to kick me in my ass.' He kept saying that, so I said, 'Okay,' and I nudged him with my knee, one of those things, and he said, 'No, no. I want you to kick me in my ass for letting myself get into this position.' So I stepped back and playfully brought my foot up, you know; I didn't kick him; nobody could kick Bird."

The second incident with the horn still distresses Jackie because it was the last time he saw Bird alive, and Jackie regrets that their relationship had not been better at the time of Bird's death. Jackie amends the story quoted below as it is told in Bob Reisner's book *The Legend of Charlie Parker,* saying that the saxophone at issue was one that both he and Parker were using, and not Jackie's exclusively: "The last time I saw him was not too pleasant. I got sick one night at a place in the Village called the Montmartre. Ahmed Basheer took me home, and Bird said he'd mind my horn. He hocked it, and I was quite angry with him. I managed to get it back in time to make a Sunday night job at the Open Door. Bird was there at a table, and I wouldn't talk to him. At closing he was outside, and he said, 'Going uptown? I'll get a cab for us.' 'I'll get my own, Bird,' I said, and did. Not long afterward I was sitting on a bus. I opened the paper and read it. I had to get off that bus. I didn't know what street, but I walked down it, crying."

One day in 1957, Jackie went to his connection and bought a couple of bags of heroin. Police had been watching the connection's house, and Jackie was arrested as he was leaving. He was given probation as a first offender, but his cabaret card was taken away. He was subsequently arrested twice again for possession of narcotics, and served a total of eleven months in jail.

Even worse than the time spent in jail was the loss of his cabaret card, as that meant that he could not work at his profession in New York City until the police department decided to reissue it. For the next seven years, during which he could obtain only temporary cards, irregularly issued, his jobs were spotty, at best. The law requiring cabaret cards issued by the police department for work in nightclubs selling liquor is a totally antiquated one which by now applies almost exclusively to jazz musicians in a most discriminatory way. It was passed after prohibition, when New York City policemen noticed that the gangland influence in the nightclubs was still strong even after the legalization of the sale of liquor. The law states in essence that persons with criminal records cannot be employed on premises that sell liquor, and at first it did give the police a *modus operandi* against the gangsters. In a few years, however, the organized criminals who were involved in nightclub operations found ways around the licensing law, and by now jazz musicians are the only ones affected by it. It is a source of graft for corrupt policemen, and musicians will tell you that two hundred dollars in the hands of a slick lawyer will get your card back for you. Although Jackie has been working through legitimate channels, by early in 1966 he still had only a temporary card. It must be re-emphasized that this is a thoroughly antiquated and discriminatory law; many lawyers feel that it is a clear violation of the constitutional right to seek gainful employment in one's chosen profession.

In 1959, Jack Gelber's play *The Connection* was presented at the now-defunct Living Theatre under the direction of Judith Malina, with décor by Julian Beck. Later made into a film by Shirley Clarke, *The Connection* is not a good play in a dramaturgical sense, as its lines are trite and its methods embarrassingly derived from Pirandello and Beckett, but it did have a certain amount of firsthand realism to it that astonished and intrigued a large enough portion of the New York theater audience to give the play the longest run of any that the Living Theatre produced during its all-too-short existence. The play deals with a group of drug addicts sitting around waiting for their connection, Cowboy (who might just as easily have been Godot, Lefty, or the Iceman), to return with the dope. Live jazz was an integral part of the play, and jazz musicians made up almost half the cast. Jackie McLean played one of the musician-junkies, and since he was barred from working in nightclubs at the time, the job was a godsend for him: "It was a steady thing, and then I enjoyed it because being in a play was a different type of thing than I had been doing, and I enjoyed making the movie, too. It was easy to do. I didn't have to portray any particular character; I could more or less just be myself up there—a musician.

"At first, the actors had no idea how to act in that particular situation. They didn't have to act like musicians, they had to act like junkies, and I guess many of them had never been around or seen junkies. But the majority of the musicians, even the ones who don't use, can mimic a junkie, and we had to show the actors how to portray them. I lost all perspective as far as the message of that play is concerned.

I was in it too long; I saw it take on many different things. One thing that I liked about it was that it wasn't the same too many nights. One night [pianist] Walter Davis would take the show, and it wouldn't be about a bunch of people waiting for the connection, it would be about a bunch of people at Walter Davis' house listening to him play the piano. Some nights it would be about the musicians playing, and other nights it would be about the kinds of things that the actors could get into. By the time we stopped playing it, we had forgotten what the original lines were, and I know it was better then than in the beginning.

"In London they booed us, catcalls and everything. It was a ridiculous play to take to London anyway. We played in the West End in London in one of those Shakespearean theaters, and the people there didn't know what the narcotic problem was about. Nobody waits for Cowboy in London; they go to their doctor and get a prescription. In London they thought it was like pornography or something."

That trip to London in 1961 with *The Connection* was Jackie's first trip out of America. When the play closed in London and the rest of the cast returned to New York, he went on to Paris, where he took a job in a club called the Chat Qui Peche. That job lasted for two months, and Jackie enjoyed it immensely. It was a different kind of alienation than he had known in New York, one that concerned him as an individual and not as a member of a group. He ran into the American Negro painter Bob Thompson, whom he had met briefly in New York City. They spent much of their time in Paris together, and Thompson introduced Jackie to the Parisian art and literary sets.

Jackie returned to New York in October of 1961 and had to rely for two years on record dates and out-of-town jobs for his income. He had signed with Blue Note records in

1959, and had recorded six records for them, all of which had sold well. Each of these records relies on the big beat that Jackie had known in Art Blakey's Jazz Messengers, and in that sense they represent a reversion for him to his pre-Mingus days. One composition, "Quadrangle," which Jackie had written in 1955, involved an elaborate group construction that he was afraid would be too far-out to release as he conceived it, so he superimposed some "I Got Rhythm" changes to make it more palatable. Leonard Feather quotes Jackie in the liner notes as saying, "I had some trouble at first putting chords to it for blowing on, but I wanted to have a firm basis to play on, as well as those figures that came into my head." Feather followed this remark with, "In other words, this is not comparable with an Ornette Coleman creation in which, after the theme has been stated, everyone takes off into outer space." But this is exactly what Jackie had conceived earlier, and he regrets today having compromised the idea, as it is the kind of composition he was to go into in the next two years. Jackie followed this penchant for the hard-bop conventions in his next recording, *A Fickle Sonance*, recorded just after he returned to New York from Paris.

But then began a reconsideration of those conventions by which Jackie had played throughout his career. Ornette Coleman, John Coltrane, and Cecil Taylor had been developing concepts that dated the hard-bop principles, and reduced simple funk to cliché. Jackie recognized the resistance to these new developments in jazz by musicians committed to hard-bop and West Coast modes as the same kind of resistance he had seen the beboppers subjected to. He also recognized a recurrence of some of the ideas Mingus had been advancing, ideas he had intended to use but had never gotten around to.

Let Freedom Ring, Jackie's second release after returning from Paris, shows a decided break with his past, and
he admitted it. He wrote the liner notes himself, and they
are confessional in nature, congratulatory in tone. In them,
Jackie acknowledged the emotive content of the new music
as the substance of the music of the Sixties, and declared
himself in favor of the break with the past.

He discarded completely the old form of twelve-bar
composition, and sectionalized his structure in a way similar
to that of Charlie Mingus. His solo work is far more aggres-
sive and uses more overtones, dissonances, and modulations
than he had played before. Equally important is the fact that
two of the three musicians Jackie used on *Let Freedom Ring*,
Herbie Lewis, the bassist, and drummer Billy Higgins
(Walter Davis, the pianist on this date, is from Jackie's
generation, but *Let Freedom Ring* is his most experimental
record), were committed to the new music. Jackie has since
recorded only with avant-garde musicians, with the exception of Roy Haynes, most flexible of drummers, whom he
considers the father of avant-garde drum playing.

Jackie's own writing and playing have developed along
the lines of *Let Freedom Ring*, and he now employs the ever-
changing polyrhythms, the extended form and the modality
that are so prominent in the new music. His conversion, if it
may be called that, gave the avant-garde an enormous boost
when most of his contemporaries were screaming "fraud." In
the early Sixties, many of the black jazz musicians in New
York lived in Brooklyn's Bedford-Stuyvesant ghetto, and
Jackie was their pace-setter. He was looked up to as a man
who had "paid his dues," taken two falls for narcotics, and
appeared on nearly one hundred recordings. Jackie's sound
had never changed, but his style had been broad enough
to include all of the various innovations that took place

during his career. So when he adapted his music to enter the avant-garde, he took with him some of the promising young musicians who had not developed a fixed concept in their own work.

One such musician was Anthony "Tony" Williams, a brilliant drummer whom Jackie met in Boston in 1962. Williams was seventeen at the time, the same age Jackie had been when he first met Bud Powell; and Jackie must have seen a piece of his own life mirrored in the young drummer. Williams went on to play with Jackie's old tutor, Miles Davis, in a group that is Miles's most exciting since the one that included John Coltrane, Bill Evans, bassist Paul Chambers, and drummer Philly Joe Jones in the late Fifties.

Trombonist Grachan Moncur III and Bobby Hutcherson, the vibist, are two young musicians whom Jackie employs often. Both are close to being the only truly new voices on their instruments since the early bebop days, when J. J. Johnson set the style for trombone playing and Milt Jackson for vibes.

Jackie's work around New York between 1961 and 1965 continued to be sporadic because of the loss of his cabaret card. Early in 1964, he made a tour of Japan with the group that included Reggie Werkman, bassist, Cedar Walton on piano, Benny Golson on tenor saxophone, and Roy Haynes on drums. He described it as "... a beautiful trip. For the first time in my life I got the feeling of what it's like to be in a country that's not dominated by the Caucasian race. It's a different feeling to go into another man's country and see a man with a closer color relationship to you running his own country and to watch the white man take the back seat, on the defense. It's a big weight off your shoulders. You don't have to worry about people looking at you funny and feeling

funny things. That was one of the biggest thrills of going to
Japan.

"And then, too, the people in Japan are so courteous
that you forget about thinking about whether they mean it
or not. I've heard cats say, 'Aw man, they bow like that
and carry on like that but they are just getting your money,'
but I don't look at it like that because they treat each other
the same way.

"There's not much of a club jazz scene going on there.
We went over to do concerts. We played in all the major
cities, and every time we'd get to an airport hundreds of
people would come out and meet us. It was like the Beatles
coming here, only not as much pandemonium and screaming. I didn't realize how many records I had made until I got
there; but there were people with all these different albums
that I was on, and albums the other guys were on, and they
had us sign their albums, sign their raincoats and shirts. They
really are devoted jazz fans."

Soon after his return to the states, Jackie lost an appeal
of a three-year-old narcotics conviction. It cost him six
months in prison, and he decided that it would be the last
time he would give a piece of his life to the state. He saw
things happen in prison that no man should have to endure:
he witnessed murderous fights between the inmates, saw
inmates brutalized by sadistic guards, and, worst of all, fair
young boys raped by older inmates who had become homo-
sexual during internment.

In looking back, Jackie sees, not a series of abrupt
breaks, but a continuum: "Miles and I were talking about
the business recently, and I was telling him that I got a little
dragged with the separation of the different [musical] con-
ceptions when it didn't have to be that way. It should just
be music for the sake of music, and people listening to what-

ever music they thought was worthwhile listening to. Cats talk about the 'New Thing' so much, but the new thing comes out of the old thing, and in a way they're part of the same thing. Take bebop, for example. First of all, I don't agree with the name. It's kind of typical, you know, you can imagine who probably thought to call it bebop. They took some of Dizzy's scat phrases, like 'oogliabopandbebop,' and they stuck on to the 'bebop.' But it was really a serious phase in music, man. It took a lot of time for people who name things to get on to bebop, but when they finally got on to it, then they tried to divide it into cool bop, cool sounds, hard bop, and all that.

"Now, to me, Lester Young played bebop. He played bebop in a different kind of setting. He didn't have bebop drummers playing with him with Basie's band, but when he played with Sid Catlett, who I think was a bebop drummer in the swing era, then you got a different kind of swing. Charlie Christian was a bebop musician, but before the term was dropped on the music; and of course Charlie Christian died before the movement reached the stage where it was called bebop. If you listen to those records he made with Monk and Klook [Kenny Clarke, the drummer] up in Minton's, then you'd see that he and the rest of them were thinking about the same thing musically that was going to come. [Bassist] Jimmy Blanton was another bebop musician in a swing setting.

"And you could call Duke a bebop musician if you wanted to, particularly if you listen to Duke's piano comping, the way he accompanies up-tempo things on the piano. I'm not thinking of his more melodic compositions like 'Sophisticated Lady,' but his conception of up-tempo things is not much different from Monk's conception. Monk's conception is derived directly from Duke, and it's beautiful to see that transition. But they take everything and put it into categories; they take Duke and put him into swing, now how can you place that man? Or how can you put jazz beyond Monk? How can you keep Monk tied into a bebop situation; it's just Monk; it isn't anything that would fit a name as terrible as bebop. If you go to hear Coltrane, it's just 'Trane and it's nobody else, and it's not any kind of movement.

"It's a little better to say that somebody is playing the saxophone who reminds you of 'Trane, to say that he's playing in 'Trane's area, or that he's very strongly influenced by Ornette Coleman or Johnny Hodges; that's better than saying he's a swing musician or a 'New Thing' musician. But then you call it the 'New Thing' and 'Third Stream' and all those things, and it gets a little tight. Like Miles said, it's just music, good or bad. If it was any different, then when you listen to Bud playing those early tunes like 'Echoes of Harlem' with Cootie Williams' band, then you'd have to say Bud was either playing swing or bebop, whichever you decided, when actually he was only playing Bud. You see?

"It's the same way now. What was 'Trane playing when he was in Miles's band? Was it hard bop or cool bop or was it 'Trane? The same way with Ornette. They hung the 'New Thing' on 'Trane as well as Ornette, but is Ornette any newer than Charlie Parker? I don't think Ornette thinks so. And why would you call music a 'Thing' anyway?"

In his own music, Jackie is now concerned only with sound, which he considers the basis of jazz: "It's not about notation, really. I imagine someone could take a chart and write down every chord or every dissonance that Monk plays, but if you played it back from that chart, then it wouldn't be Monk. It wouldn't sound anything like him. So when you start dealing with sounds, you either have to go by your ear, like I'm going, or you have to become a scientist and start measuring all the vibrations and all that kind of stuff."

Early in 1966, Jackie worked in the Arts and Culture program at HARYOU-ACT.* The organization has a large jazz program with one of the best teen-age bands in the country; Jackie's son, Rene, an excellent young alto saxophonist who has obviously been influenced by his father, is a featured soloist with the band. Jackie suggested to the director of the Arts and Culture program that it might be better to enlarge the jazz program into a complete music department, with sections for chorus, voice training, jazz, steel band, harmony and theory, composition, and the like. He was then asked to organize and supervise the new department, with a promise that he would be given the job of director if the program could be funded, a rare demonstration of perception and understanding on the part of an organization's administrators. Soon, however, he was caught in a bureaucratic upheaval that resulted in the dismissal of the head of the Arts and Culture program and the scrapping of all of her projects, including the music department.

With the dwindling number of nightclubs that employ jazz musicians, Jackie, like most members of his profession, feels that new scenes have to be created. He does not see the total disappearance of the jazz club: "Jazz is a party music; I know that when I play jazz I'm always partying, and I think that's an element that shouldn't go out of it." He thinks the least America can do would be to provide a large federal subsidy for jazz musicians: "I think that the United States, to make up for what happened to Charlie Parker, and to

* The combination of Harlem Youth Opportunities Unlimited, Inc., and Associated Community Teams, Inc., the federally sponsored anti-poverty unit designed to positively channel the energies of youth in New York's black ghettoes.

make sure that there are no more Charlie Parkers—that is, no more geniuses going to waste like Charlie Parker did, should subsidize jazz. Jazz is the only true art form that this country has come up with, since the U.S. certainly did not produce classical music nor any art form except jazz, and maybe the atomic bomb. This country should make sure that young musicians are paid, as they are in the HARYOU-ACT Anti-Poverty Program. If I had had an outlet like that, maybe I wouldn't have had such a tough time. I know that wouldn't answer the whole problem, but it would be a beginning."

Jackie sees in his son Rene an advancement from the time that he was struggling in the streets of Harlem: "Kids come up today knowing a lot more. I did meet a couple of artists when I was a kid—for example, Ollie Harrington, who used to draw Bootsie in the *Amsterdam News,* and Beuford Delaney, the Negro painter who lives in Paris now. But I didn't know anywhere near as many as Rene knows already. You ask Rene about Charlie Parker and he and all his friends can tell you about him. He also knows about drugs and that whole scene. He doesn't have to go around being hip."

INDEX